THE BIRTH OF JESUS

D1545976

BISHOP JOHN SHELBY SPONG

PROGRESSIVE
CHRISTIANITY.ORG
Gig Harbor, WA

Contents

v

Preface

It has been a pleasure and an honor to have had the opportunity to publish the Bishop John Shelby Spong weekly essays for our subscribers over the last three years. During that time we have had, and continue to have, requests for printed versions of the Spong essays. After careful study we determined it would be financially prohibitive to produce and mail printed copies on a regular basis. However, as we reviewed all the essays, we concluded it would be possible to group together some of the essays as a series and publish them in a booklet form. That is what we have done here with the essays dealing with the birth stories of Jesus.

We started with the birth series because no series has generated more comments from our readers. As one subscriber wrote, "It all starts with the birth story—get that wrong and we probably get it all wrong." No one does a better job of getting it right than John Shelby Spong. And there is always the added bonus with Bishop Spong. He is the consummate teacher. He writes with the primary intention for readers, regardless of their training or background, to get it.

While Luke's narrative, the most detailed account of the birth of Jesus, is lyrical and inspiring, Spong persuasively demonstrates it is allegory. Layer by layer, Spong weighs every element of the New Testament stories against Old Testament legends building a convincing case.

Zachariah and Elizabeth, for example, are childless into old age until she conceives John, forerunner to Jesus. This mirrors the story of Abraham and Sarah whose son, Isaac, was born when Abraham was 99-years old. Spong's essays step backward and forward through the scriptures demonstrating why each element was chosen by the early CE writers to establish Jesus' lineage and divinity. It is a fascinating and persuasive journey and a remarkable illustration of Biblical scholarship.

It is our sincere hope that this project will not only satisfy the regular subscribers who continue to ask us for printed materials but will also allow us to reach a new audience not yet familiar with Spong's work. We believe his work continues to break new ground pointing the way to a new understanding of the Jesus story and as a result a new Christianity for the 21st century.

We look forward to your continued support, your comments and feedback about this new project.

Fred Plumer
President
ProgressiveChristianity.org

The Legend Revisited

Most of the portraits of the mother of Jesus that hang in the great museums of the world are dependent first on the biblical stories of Jesus' birth and second on the presumed appearances of his mother at the foot of the cross. Take those two traditions away from the New Testament and the mother of Jesus almost totally disappears. Indeed, what remains is mostly negative. She is portrayed in Mark (chapters 3 and 6) as thinking Jesus was beside himself, that is out of his mind. She, along with his brothers, moves to put him away. This story implies he had become an embarrassment to the family. In the Fourth Gospel, in the narrative of the water being changed into wine, the mother of Jesus is portrayed as inappropriately pushing Jesus to act. She receives from him the rebuke, "Woman, what have you to do with me, my hour has not yet come?" She is also not present at the cross in the writings of Paul or in any of the earlier gospels of Mark, Matthew or Luke. Only with the appearance of the Fourth Gospel at the end of the first century did anyone think to portray her at the foot of the cross.

These biblical facts force us to recognize that most of the ideas we have about the mother of Jesus are late developing myths making assumptions the Bible does not make. The birth stories are found first in Matthew, the dating of which is generally between 82 and 85. Second they are found in Luke which is generally thought to have been written about a decade after Matthew. This means the New Testament accounts of Jesus' birth are products of a time 52–65 years after the life of Jesus came to its earthly end. This was some 82–95 years after the time of his birth. This is not eye witness reporting. Clearly the tradition built around the mother of Jesus is both late developing and continues to grow with the passing of years.

Once the time of the writing of the New Testament has passed, however, the mythology that developed around the mother of Jesus apparently knew no bounds. The virgin mother of the birth narratives became in successive generations the permanent virgin. Thus Jesus' siblings, referred to by name in both Galatians and in Mark and John simply as his brothers, were redefined as half brothers or cousins. Further, she was declared to have been a postpartum virgin. This suggests that even the birth of Jesus did not disturb her virginal hymen.

In the service of that idea the Fathers of the church searched the scriptures for biblical texts to support this growing conviction. They settled on two. First, they looked at the writings of a sixth century BCE prophet named Ezekiel. In the first verse of the 44th chapter he wrote these words: "This gate shall remain shut; it shall not be opened and no one shall enter by it, for the Lord, the God of Israel, has entered by it; therefore it shall remain shut." Without either apology or embarrassment, they leaped on these words to claim the post partum virginity of the Blessed Virgin Mary had actually been predicted by the prophets.

The second text was found in the resurrection story according to the Fourth Gospel. In that narrative the disciples were hiding in an upper room. The doors and windows were closed and locked when Jesus came and stood in their midst. If the risen Christ could pass through walls guarded by locked doors, they argued, it was no great stretch to imagine the infant Christ passing through the birth canal of his mother without breaking the hymen. Mythology always does strange things to facts and to reality.

By the 19th century, devotion to the mother of Jesus grew even stronger in the Roman Catholic Church in which this devotion was most encouraged. She, unlike all other human beings, had been immaculately conceived it was declared. That is, her mother had been miraculously cleansed of the sin of Adam. This was believed to have infected all human beings and to have been passed on from generation to generation. For Jesus to have been born without sin, his mother would have to have been especially prepared for this birth.

This necessity also reflected the discovery in the early years of the 18th century that women have an egg cell. Therefore the woman literally contributes half of the genetic makeup of every person who has ever been born. Prior to this it was assumed the woman simply provided a womb to nurture the male seed to maturity. Like Mother Earth into which the farmer planted the seed, the woman's role was simply seen as to bring to birth the life that came from the male. When the egg cell was discovered, the realization dawned on church leadership that the mother of Jesus, like all women—and indeed like all people—was a child of Adam. Thus the sinlessness of Jesus was compromised through his mother's line. This had not been a problem in the old view of reproduction. The Immaculate Conception addressed that theological problem. This demonstrated once and for all that even infallible doctrines are forced to adjust to new discoveries.

The final chapter in the mythological development of the mother of Jesus came in the 20th century when Mary was declared to have been bodily assumed into heaven. Since she was born without sin, she was not required to go through the passage of death. According to the story of the Garden of Eden, death was punishment for sin.

Carl Jung rejoiced in the Vatican's declaration of the bodily assumption of the mother of Jesus into heaven. In his world of symbols this meant the feminine had finally been lifted into God. The patriarchal tyranny of a God conceived of in only masculine terms and always addressed as Father had finally been tempered.

In this undertaking, first I want to get underneath the mythology of the ages. Second, I want to trace the story development found in the New Testament itself. Then we can look at Jesus, the mother of Jesus and the entire Christian story with new eyes. Honed by scholarship and tempered by the facts of history as we can demonstrate them, I trust it will be an illuminating and worthwhile story.

If the familiar biblical images of the mother of Jesus are late developing, what is original and perhaps trustworthy? That is the question we will address as this story unfolds. I begin with some statements of fact I will pursue in detail going into each of them deeply before any conclusions are reached. For now, I simply file them as bullet points for your consideration. As the Book of Common Prayer in my church states these bullet points are designed to be "read, marked, learned and inwardly digested." This series will provide the time to do just that.

We can now date the life of Jesus with some degree of accuracy. Recent discoveries have made it possible to fix the life of Jesus between the years of 4 BCE and 30 CE. We get to these dates first by the discovery in ancient Roman records that King Herod died in 4 BCE. The clear New Testament tradition is that Jesus was born when Herod was the king so we fix the date of Jesus birth at 4 BCE. Second, we learn, once more from secular records, that Pilate was the procurator of Judea for the Roman Empire between the years 26–36 CE. If, as each of the gospels asserts, the crucifixion occurred under the authority of Pilate, then the crucifixion has to happen sometime between those dates. Roman records also provide us with some other facts in the life of

Pilate having to do with the reasons for his removal from office. Since they appear to have happened well after the crucifixion, we can squeeze those dates a bit closer to perhaps 28–32 as the time of the crucifixion. We then split the difference and settle on 30 CE knowing we might be off two years in either direction. For our working purposes, we set the life of Jesus between 4 BC and 30 CE.

We have nothing preserved in writing anywhere of anything concerning the life of Jesus before the year 51 CE. This silent and dark historical tunnel can be illumined only by speculation. It is filled in only by what we call oral tradition which we have almost no way of recreating, entering or capturing.

Paul, the first writer whose work was destined to be included in the New Testament, did all of his writing between the years 51 and 64 CE. Not all of the epistles attributed to Paul are authentically from his hand. The ones which have earned a consensus on the certainty of Pauline authorship are I Thessalonians, Galatians, I and II Corinthians, Romans, Philemon and Philippians. This means II Thessalonians, Colossians, Ephesians, I and II Timothy, Titus and Hebrews are not considered to be from the hand of Paul.

Nowhere, in any part of the authentic Pauline corpus, is there a reference of any kind to the birth of Jesus, nor is there any mention of the mother or father of Jesus. There are in Paul, however, several references, mostly in Galatians, to James, the brother of the Lord.

Our study of the birth of Jesus will therefore start with Paul, the earliest writer in the New Testament. That means we will start our investigation in the sixth and seventh decades of the Christian era.

Paul and the Virgin Birth

In the writings of Paul there is not a single reference to a supernatural birth tradition regarding Jesus of Nazareth. This fact is easily established. Determining what it means is a bit more complicated.

Does this omission mean Paul was unaware of this part of the Christian tradition? Is it possible a story as dramatic as the one appearing 20–30 years later in the gospels of Matthew and Luke could have been ignored by Paul if it had been known? Paul was an educated man. The idea of a great person being born in a supernatural way that pre-saged his greatness was not unknown. For example, there were birth legends surrounding the nativity of such icons as Alexander the great, Romulus and Remus and the deity called Mithra. All of them were almost certainly known by Paul. So the evidence suggests Paul did not include any reference to this tradition in regard to Jesus' birth because he had never heard of it. If Paul had never heard of this tradition, the overwhelmingly probable explanation would be that the miraculous stories of Jesus' birth had not yet been written. This means they were not an original part of the Christian story. However, as an argument from silence, it is not regarded as particularly definitive. So we turn to Paul's writings to see what might be possible for us to conclude as the reality he knew on this subject.

Paul gives us some biographical details in the Epistle to the Galatians, one of his earliest epistles. Here he argues the gospel he proclaims "is not man's (nor according to man) gospel." He goes on to say, "I did not receive it from man nor was I taught it but it came through a revelation of Jesus Christ" (Gal. 1:10–12). Then he recites his history as a persecutor of the Christian Church. Obviously that was well known. However, the details of his conversion on the road to Damascus will not be written until Luke produced the Book of Acts in the tenth decade of the Common Era. This was some 30 plus years after the death of Paul.

Paul then describes his life in Judaism in which he asserts he was "extremely zealous" for "the tradition of my fathers" (Gal. 1:14). Then he described his conversion saying God had "set me apart" and was "pleased to reveal his son to me in order that I might preach him among the Gentiles."

To back up this claim, Paul says that after his conversion, which scholars place between one and six years following the crucifixion, he went to Arabia for three years. Only then did he go up to Jerusalem to visit Cephus, that is Peter, and stayed with him for 15 days. He says he saw no other apostle "except for James, the Lord's brother." So at some time no earlier than four years and no later than nine years after the crucifixion, Paul was in the presence of Peter and James, the brother of Jesus. In the first epistle to the Corinthians in chapter 11 and in chapter 15, Paul uses the phrase, "For I received from the Lord what I also delivered to you." In chapter 11 that phrase introduces Paul's understanding of the institution of the Lord's Supper. In chapter 15 he relates the final events in Jesus' life: the crucifixion, the burial and the Easter experience of resurrection.

From putting these events together we know Paul learned many of the details of the Jesus story from his association with the disciples. However, Paul insists he got to know Jesus directly by way of a revelatory experience.

He also knows Jesus had a brother. If the miraculous birth of Jesus had been a fact of history instead of a later developing legend, it seems obvious an event of this presumed degree of importance would have been communicated to Paul. It wasn't. In none of Paul's writings is there any mention of the mother of Jesus, the father of Jesus or the birth of Jesus.

This still remains an argument from silence and as such continues to be weak and inconclusive. So, back to the Epistle to the Galatians we go in search of more data. Here we discover Paul actually discusses the origins of Jesus. Interpreting the differences in being a child in a family as opposed to being a slave in a family, he argues that children are heirs. Even though they are placed under the authority of guardians, teachers and trustees until they come of age, they are nonetheless destined for freedom and their inheritance. Paul uses this analogy to explain the role of the law given to the people of Israel. The law is to them what guardians, teachers and trustees are to children who are not yet of age. They are obedient to them while they wait for their promised inheritance. In Paul's mind, the role of Jesus was to give to all human life, Jews and Gentiles alike, the inheritance of full humanity. This is called sonship in the patriarchal world. Then in a wonderfully clear affirmation, Paul asserts, "When the time had fully come, God sent forth his son, born of a woman, born under the law, so we might receive adoption as sons." (Gal. 4:8).

For Paul, Jesus was born of a woman. That is, he was born just like any other person. It is not possible, he was suggesting, to be born in any other way. Could the word translated as woman have in it any connotation of virgin? Not a chance. The Greek word used here is a form of the word gunos from which we get the word gynecology. It is not the word parthenos from which we get the word parthenogenesis. This is to give birth by a single sex and does include the connotation of virgin. Jesus came from God the way every life comes from God, he was born of a woman. Like every Jew, Paul says, Jesus was also born under the law. Paul could not be clearer. The idea of a miraculous or virgin birth is never hinted at by this early Christian writer because he had never heard of it. The story of Jesus' supernatural birth had not yet been written or developed.

When these birth stories were written, one of their purposes was to assert that from the moment of his birth, Jesus was uniquely related to God. It is also clear this idea was not one entertained by Paul. To make this case we turn to the opening verses of the Epistle to the Romans.

Paul certainly gives expression to his conviction that somehow and through some means, the reality of God they thought of as transcendent had been experienced as present in Jesus of Nazareth. In his early epistles he was content to simply proclaim the reality of this experience not to explain it. So he wrote that "God was in Christ." The content that made this claim real was the experience of reconciliation. In the Christ experience, those people who had once been separated are brought together. In Galatians, the apostle again proclaims that inside the Christ experience, human differences and human barriers simply fade away. In Christ, there is no such thing as tribal identity. There is no Jew or Greek, no Jew or Gentile, but one humanity. In Christ, there is no gender identity, no male or female, but a single humanity. In Christ, value is not established by economic or social standards, there is no bond or free, no slave or master, but a new creation, a new oneness. That was the God experience Paul found in Jesus.

This theme resonated throughout the New Testament. We see it in the Pentecost story of Acts 2 where spirit-filled people are said to be able to communicate in the same language of human oneness. We see it in the divine commission in Matthew 28 where the followers of Jesus are instructed in the name of Jesus to go to those whom they have previously described as unclean and unworthy and to proclaim to them the limitless love of God. We see it in the Fourth Gospel in which Jesus defines his purpose as giving abundant life to all. That is the God experience his followers believed they had met in Jesus. When did this God presence enter into Jesus? Paul says it was at the time of the resurrection. This was the moment in which God and Jesus became one in the mind of Paul. To the Romans Paul writes that Jesus was descended from King David "according to the flesh," but was "designated Son of God in power according to the spirit of holiness by his resurrection from the dead" (Romans 1:3–4).

As the tradition developed, the moment when God and Jesus became part of each other would get earlier and earlier. In Mark it was when he was baptized. In Matthew and Luke, it was when he was conceived. In John it was at the dawn of creation. The story of the origins of Jesus' power would develop significantly between Paul and the later gospels. In that later development, the story of the Virgin Birth would be born and it would begin to grow. Paul, however, knew nothing of this tradition since it was not developed until well after his death.

The witness of Paul is clear. He never heard of the Virgin Birth. This fact begins to qualify the power of this claim as revealed truth. The Virgin Birth is not an essential ingredient in the Christian story. Why? Because one can hardly say Paul, who had never heard of the Virgin Birth tradition, was not a Christian.

The Testimony of Mark, the Earliest Gospel

The first gospel to be written, the one we call Mark, was composed in the early years of the 8th decade (70–72). It contains no story of and no reference to the birth of Jesus. To explain this omission there are only two possibilities. Either the author of Mark had never heard about the birth tradition because it had not yet been created or he knew about it and deemed it unworthy of inclusion. For a number of reasons the first of these two alternatives is generally agreed to be the overwhelming probability.

First of all, it is not just an argument from silence. There are a number of episodes in the corpus of Mark's gospel that would have been either impossible or incomprehensible if he had been aware of a miraculous birth tradition. I will look at three of them.

In the first chapter of this gospel we find the familiar story of Jesus coming to John the Baptist to be baptized. The preamble to this episode is not a birth story or a childhood story. It is a reference to the fact that Jesus was believed to be the fulfillment of the hopes and the writings of the prophets. Mark builds this case by quoting Malachi 3:1 and II Isaiah 40:3, although he only acknowledges his dependence on Isaiah in the text. Then he launches into a description of John the Baptist developed in such a way as to identify him with the prophet Elijah. Mark describes John the Baptist as wearing the clothing of Elijah, a man of the desert. He portrays him as eating Elijah's diet of locusts and wild honey (Mark 1:6–7 and II Kings 1:8). By turning John the Baptist into an Elijah-like figure, Mark was playing to the messianic images suggesting Elijah must come first to prepare the way for the messiah. John the Baptist has thus been designated by Mark to play this role in the first gospel to appear in writing. This is not history. This is interpretive portrait painting. The synagogue audience for whom Mark was writing would immediately understand the symbols he was employing.

Next, in the first act Mark attributes to Jesus, he is baptized by John in the Jordan River. There is nothing about this gospel's first mention of Jesus to suggest he was different or supernatural because of some aspect of his birth. He was pictured simply as an adult, a fully human male. Mark employed the custom of that day by introducing Jesus by name followed by his home town. If any further identification was needed, Mark would have said, "Jesus of Nazareth, the son of ____" and then named his father. That was not deemed necessary for Mark's introduction. Indeed, the father of Jesus, whether human or divine, is never mentioned in this gospel.

It is only in this account of his baptism that the first supernatural references are mentioned by this writer. First, he said, the heavens opened. The sky was thought of as a dome separating the realm of God above from the realm of human life below. In the creation story, which would have been quite familiar to Mark's Jewish audience (Genesis 1:6), the sky was called the firmament. It was supposed to have served to separate "the waters above from the waters below." The heavenly waters falling from the sky as rain formed the earthly waters that became the oceans, rivers and streams. In time, that heavenly water came to be identified with the Holy Spirit. So in this narrative the heavens opened to the dwelling place of God and the Spirit descended from God to fall on Jesus like a dove.

Then a voice from heaven rang out across the earth proclaiming Jesus to be God's "beloved Son, with whom I am well pleased." Once again in the use of these words, texts from the Hebrew Scriptures were in the mind of the writer of this gospel. In Isaiah, God referred to the "suffering servant" as "My chosen in whom my soul delights" (Is. 42:1). The Psalter has God refer to the Lord's anointed as, "You are my son, today have I begotten you" (Ps. 7:2). The Spirit does not come on Jesus just for a season, but has come to dwell on him permanently. Thus, he becomes a God-infused human life.

The Holy Spirit was not the male agent in conception as the later birth narratives would assert. The Holy Spirit dropped from heaven on the fully human adult Jesus at this baptism to indwell him in an ongoing manner. This was Mark's way of explaining the source of the divine presence found in Jesus. Had he known about the virgin birth tradition, Mark's explanation of the coming of the Spirit to dwell permanently in him would not have been necessary. The later developing supernatural story of Jesus' miraculous birth had clearly not yet been thought of or composed by anyone.

The second Marcan episode revealing he had never heard the story of the virgin birth comes in chapter 3. Jesus, we are told, has broken onto the public scene in a series of rapid-fire activities. He had chosen some disciples; astonished a congregation at Capernaum with his teaching in a synagogue; and healed a man with an unclean spirit, who then with supernatural insight, recognized Jesus' divine presence. He healed Peter's mother-in-law, cast out demons and healed the sick of an entire city, cleansed a leper, healed a paralytic and called Levi from his tax collecting trade into discipleship. He distinguished himself from John the Baptist, violated the Sabbath by picking and eating grain in the fields and proclaimed himself Lord of the Sabbath. Finally, in the synagogue, he healed a man with a withered hand on the Sabbath (see chapters 2 and 3). This Sabbath healing was not an emergency act which would have made it legitimate since the hand would still be withered on the day after the Sabbath. It was a calculated Sabbath violation. All of these provocative acts attracted immediate public notice.

Then Jesus went home to Nazareth and his family began to hear of these things. They were not pleased, Mark says. "They went out to seize him, for all the people were saying, 'He is beside himself'" (Mark 3:20–21). This is the first biblical mention of the family of Jesus other than Paul's reference to James as the brother of the Lord in Galatians. It is not, however, until the end of this chapter when the family of Jesus is defined. Thinking him mentally disturbed, which is what the words beside himself mean, Mark tells us "Jesus' mother and his brothers came to where he was." Standing outside the crowd, they sent a message to him asking him to come out. When informed of their presence, Jesus not only declined to accede to their wishes, but he also redefined his kinship to them. Whoever does "the will of God," he said, "is my brother and sister and mother." (Mark 3:35)

Note that the mother of Jesus thinks him mentally disturbed. This is not the behavior of one to whom an angel might have appeared to tell her she would be the mother of the messiah. One does not receive that divine message prior to a child's birth and then think he has gone out of his mind when he reaches his adult life. When Mark wrote this gospel he had not heard of the tradition that Jesus had a supernatural birth because it had not yet been created.

The final Marcan episode making it clear the birth narrative of Jesus was not part of the original Christian tradition, but a late-developing addition to the story, comes in the sixth chapter of Mark. Jesus had returned to his home in Nazareth from a series of adventures described in chapters 4 and 5. This included casting a legion of demons out of a demented man. Allowing these demons to enter a herd of swine caused a stampede that resulted in the drowning of the herd in the Sea of Galilee. He raised Jairus' daughter from the dead and healed the woman with the chronic menstrual flow. The author of this gospel clearly meant to suggest that the people were talking of his power and wondering about its source.

At this point, Mark says, Jesus entered his synagogue and created astonishment at his teaching. The people, who had been his neighbors, could not believe what they were hearing. So Mark had an anonymous member of the crowd ask this question: "Is not this the carpenter, the son of Mary and the brother of James, Joses, Judas and Simon and are not his sisters here with us?" (Mark 6:3–4) Please note the following things about this passage. This is the first time in the Christian story the role of the carpenter has been mentioned. It is Jesus who is cast in that role, not Joseph. That will change when we come to Matthew a decade later when the shift is made. Second, this is also the first and only time in Mark we hear Mary is the name of Jesus' mother. Third, there is no mention of a father in this family. In addition to his mother, four brothers are named. The plural word sisters is used indicating there were more than one. Finally, be aware that for an anonymous voice in the crowd to call a grown man named Jesus the son of Mary was pejorative in Jewish society. One did not call a mature man the son of a woman unless his paternity was suspect. This phrase meant his father was unknown. It thus suggests Jesus was base born or illegitimate. Rumors to this effect were clearly beginning to swirl around Jesus and echoes of these charges can be found in the other gospels. These rumors would in time create the necessity for developing the virgin birth tradition, but that time had not yet come

It is clear the first gospel writer, Mark, had never heard of the virgin birth. When Mark was written, over 40 years had passed since the crucifixion and some 70 years had passed since the birth of Jesus. Mythological traditions build slowly. The story of the virgin birth of Jesus is one of these mythological traditions.

The Two Versions of the Birth Story

The familiar stories of Jesus' miraculous birth entered the Christian tradition in two different forms separated by perhaps a decade. The original narrative was written by a man we have named Matthew somewhere between 82 and 85. The later narrative was written by a man we call Luke somewhere between 89 and 93. The second story is by far the more familiar one, primarily, I suspect, because it is dramatized annually in our Christmas pageants. The typical pageant follows the story line of Luke from the annunciation of Mary, to her visit to Elizabeth, to the journey to Bethlehem. Then there is the inn in which no room was found and angels proclaiming the messiah's birth to a group of hillside shepherds who go in search of the promised child. With this entire cast of characters in place, usually portrayed around a stable, the pageant closes by tacking on the visit of the wise men, a scene lifted out of Matthew's gospel. This combination is so deeply rooted in the minds of most people they are surprised to learn the two biblical stories of the birth of Jesus are in deep conflict with each other in a variety of details.

In Matthew there is a star in the East and a group of people called magi or wise men who follow the star in search of its meaning. In Luke there is no mention of a star or of wise men. Instead, Luke tells us of a vision of angels appearing to hillside shepherds near the village of Bethlehem who inform them of the birth of the messiah.

Armed with only the two clues the angels provided, these shepherds went to seek out this child. They had been told the babe would be wrapped in swaddling clothes and laid in a feeding trough called a manger. Miraculously, they found him and made known abroad what had been told them by the angels.

In Matthew, the magi go first to the palace of King Herod in Jerusalem to inquire of him where the new king of Israel could be found. Troubled by this visit, King Herod assembled the chief priests and scribes to determine where the messiah was to be born. They consult the Hebrew Scriptures and fasten on a text found in the prophet Micah. This suggests Bethlehem, a village less than six miles from Jerusalem, was destined to be the messianic birthplace. The magi then resume their journey, now to Bethlehem. They are led once again by the mysterious star. When they reach the exact location, it appears to stop and to bathe the house in which this birth has occurred with its bright unearthly light.

Herod asked these complete strangers to act as his central intelligence agency. He tells them to report back to him when they have located this child who presents a potential threat to his throne. However, he waits in vain for their return. The magi, having been warned by God in a dream not to return to Herod, leave for their homes by a different route. Herod, we are told, miffed by their disobedience to his command, fell into a furious rage. He dispatched his soldiers to Bethlehem with orders to kill all the boy babies up to two years of age. The tradition has called those baby boys The Holy Innocents. This presumed threat to the life of Jesus forces Joseph, who was also warned of this peril in a dream, to flee with the child and his mother to Egypt for safety.

Not a single one of these narrative details is mentioned in Luke and no Christmas pageant ever portrays the killing of these babies. Even though it is in the Bible, it is not regarded as a suitable story for the Christmas season.

While Matthew has the holy family fleeing to Egypt, Luke portrays them as having the child circumcised on the eighth day and giving him the name Jesus. Next on the 40th day, the day for the presentation, Mary and Joseph take the infant Jesus to the Temple, presumably in Jerusalem. In that setting Luke introduces an old priest named Simeon and a prophetess named Anna into the narrative. Only then do the members of the holy family make their quite leisurely way back to their home in Nazareth of Galilee.

Comparing the two narratives makes us aware of the differences between Matthew's birth story and Luke's. They are mutually contradictory. Matthew portrays Mary and Joseph as residents in the city of Bethlehem. They live there in a house where the baby is born and over which a star will shine. When this family flees from Herod, they are said to have gone to Egypt. When the threat is over, they are able to return to their home in Bethlehem.

However, this location of the holy family in Bethlehem presents Matthew with a problem. Surely, he knew Jesus was referred to in his lifetime as Jesus of Nazareth. The Galilean origins of this man are deep in the tradition. Matthew has to develop a story line that will get Jesus out of Bethlehem, the place of his birth, and into Nazareth, the place of his upbringing and identity. Matthew accomplishes this by suggesting the threat Herod made on the life of the infant Jesus was still present in Herod's son, Archelaus. Joseph, always cast in the role of Jesus' protector, is thus warned to flee to Galilee. He does so and settles in the town of Nazareth.

Matthew, who portrays every detail of Jesus' infancy as the fulfillment of scripture's expectations, asserts that moving to Nazareth fulfilled the prophetic expectation that Jesus would be called a Nazarene. This is a real stretch because no one can locate a text that includes such a designation. Perhaps it was a play on the word for a Hebrew holy man, known as a nazirene. They did not drink wine or strong drink and did not cut their hair as in the story of Samson. That designation, however, had nothing to do with living in the town of Nazareth. Another possibility is he was referring to the idea that the messiah would be born out of the root of Jesse, who was the father of King David (Isaiah 11:10). The Hebrew word for root is nazir.

On the other hand, Luke assumed Mary and Joseph lived in Nazareth. According to Luke, the annunciation to Mary occurred in the town of Nazareth. Like Matthew, however, Luke wanted to honor the tradition that the messiah, as an heir to the throne of David, had to be born in Bethlehem, the place of David's birth. Luke had to come up with a story line that would get Mary and Joseph to Bethlehem to make it possible for Jesus to be born there. His way of accomplishing this was to suggest that a census or enrollment had been ordered by Caesar Augustus. It required everyone in the empire to be counted. Luke goes on to say this enrollment occurred when Quirinius was governor of Syria. It also carried the stipulation that everyone had to return to his or her ancestral home for this census. For Joseph, and presumably for Mary, this meant they had to return to their family's place of origin. Since Joseph was of the house and lineage of David, he had to return to Bethlehem with his betrothed who was, in the lovely language of the King James Bible, great with child.

There are a number of problems with this story line. First, there is no evidence anywhere of a government program requiring a return to one's ancestral home. No one kept records that went back 1000 years, the approximate time between King David and the birth of Jesus. Second, secular records reveal that King Herod died in 4 BCE. Quirinius did not become governor of Syria until the winter of 6–7 CE. If Jesus was born when Herod was king, which Luke asserts in chapter 1:5, he would have been 10 or 11 by the time Quirinius became governor.

Third, the Hebrew Scriptures indicate King David had multiple wives. The exact number is not given but the guesses range up to 300. If you count a generation as 20 years, it was 50 generations from David to Jesus. In 50 generations the direct heirs of King David would have numbered more than a billion people. If all David's direct heirs had been required to journey to Bethlehem to be enrolled, there would certainly have been no room in the inn.

Fourth, the distance between Nazareth and Bethlehem was approximately 94 miles. To navigate it by foot or on a donkey, which were the only two methods of transportation open to them, it was a seven to ten-day trip. If Mary had been great with child, as Luke suggests, it is safe to assume she must have been in her eighth or ninth month of pregnancy.

The literal accuracy of both narratives falls apart on close examination of the two radically inconsistent and contradictory texts. They cannot both be true. The probability is that neither is true. They are interpretive narratives intended to say Jesus was the designated messiah from the moment of his birth.

We will examine in detail first the original birth story according to Matthew and then the second birth story, the familiar one, written by Luke. The deeper we go into these texts, the more fascinating they become.

Matthew's Original Story, the Prologue; and Tamar, the Incestuous One

Matthew is the gospel writer (CE 82–85) who first introduced the story of Jesus' miraculous or virgin birth
into the tradition. He did so with the 17 most boring verses
in the entire Bible. (See Matt. 1:1–17) They are Matthew's
version of the genealogy of Jesus, but we refer to them as
the who-begat-whom verses. Yet, while incredibly tedious,
I am convinced we can discover clues revealing both why
the virgin birth story was developed in the first place and
why it seems to be of such importance to the author of this
second gospel to be written.

First, some comments on the genealogy in general.
Matthew began his description of the line he claimed produced Jesus with Abraham, the traditional father of the
Jewish nation. Matthew was himself a deeply committed
Jewish writer, probably a scribe. He was writing for a traditional Jewish faith community. Therefore he was very
interested in grounding the Jesus story in the very DNA
of Jewish life and history. So he made Abraham, the first
pivotal person in Jewish history, the first pivotal person in
Jesus' lineage. David, who originated the royal family that
ruled some portion of the Hebrew nation for between 400
and 500 years, became his second pillar in Jesus' ancestry.

The next historical marker in Jesus background reflected in this genealogy was what is called the Exile. The
citizens of Judah, first in 596 BCE and finally in 586 BCE,
after being defeated by the Babylonians, were marched

into the land of their conquerors. They spent this period of Jewish history, known as the Babylonian captivity, as an underclass of laborers. This Exile lasted for two to three generations and was the time in history when the life of the Jewish nation quite literally hung by a thread. The last period covered by Matthew's genealogy was from the Exile to the birth of Jesus.

Matthew suggested each of these epochs in Jewish history had been 14 generations long. This is the point at which every shred of literal accuracy people like to attribute to this gospel begins to break down. Abraham, if he lived at all, would be dated around the year 1850 BCE. David became king of the nation, first in Hebron, about the year 1000 and seven years later in Jerusalem, his newly-conquered capitol. So, between Abraham and David, there are some 850 years. If a generation is considered to be 20 years, which actually might be far too long in that time when life expectancy did not exceed 40 years, there would have been 42 generations between Abraham and David. The time from King David to the Exile would be 400 years plus or some 20 generations. The time from the Exile to the birth of Jesus would have been around 600 years or some 30 generations. So Matthew's scheme for dividing Jewish history into the stages he wishes to describe breaks down quickly. To achieve his 14 generation mathematical symmetry, Matthew literally had to omit the names of some of the kings in Judah who reigned between David and the Exile who are described in the Hebrew Bible.

The next problem gives a biblical commentator pause with this genealogy. It goes from Abraham to David to Joseph to demonstrate Jesus' royal lineage as a son of David. When he arrives at the virgin birth story, his narrative completely denies the role of paternity to Joseph in the life of Jesus. The Virgin Birth story says Joseph, the presumed male agent in conception, was replaced by the

Holy Spirit. So this elaborate effort to ground Jesus in the life of the Jewish people is compromised by the account of his miraculous birth. Literalism wobbles visibly.

Another unusual detail in what Matthew portrays as the lineage of Jesus was the inclusion of the names of four women in the genealogy. In this patriarchal world that was quite unusual. Women were not thought to be equal partners in the procreation process. In that day, no one knew women produced an egg cell and were biologically co-creators of every baby who had ever been born. Women were rather thought of only as nurturing wombs into which males placed the seeds of life. Women simply brought them to maturity.

Yet Matthew included four women in this genealogy. They were not mythical women either. The story of each of these women can be found chronicled in the pages of the Hebrew Scriptures. Their stories were known. Even if they had not been known, anyone could go to the Bible and read about them. There was another fascinating reality about these women. By the standards of the day, each of them was considered and defined as a morally compromised woman. Please listen to the drama being presented here. In this 17 verse genealogy with which Matthew introduced the story of the Virgin Birth, he made the claim that four of the women in the line that produced Jesus of Nazareth, were what his generation would have called unclean or scandalous women. What do you imagine was Matthew's purpose in opening his story this way?

The first of these shady ladies was Tamar. Her story can be found in Genesis, chapter 38. She was the wife of Er, the first born son of the patriarch Judah. Judah had two other sons, Onan and Shelah, a fact that becomes important as the story unfolds. This chapter tells us Er was "wicked in the sight of the Lord and the Lord slew him." (Gen. 38:7). Under the law governing widows in Hebrew history, it thus became the duty of Onan, the next oldest son, to marry the wife of his deceased brother in order "to raise up offspring for your brother." (Gen. 38:8). Onan objected and practiced a primitive kind of birth control that came to be called Onanism. This act displeased God, according to this story, and so we are told God also killed Onan. Now it became Shelah's turn to marry his brother's widow, but Shelah was only a boy of about five years of age. Having seen what happened to his two older brothers when they were married to Tamar, he was eager to avoid this fate.

So Judah violated the code of behavior and the demands of the Torah and sent Tamar back to her family of origin to live under her father's protection. In this patriarchal society, Tamar was now damaged goods and she would no longer be thought of as marriageable. Judah, seeking to perfume his behavior, promised to send for her when Shelah grew up.

Some time passed during which Shelah did grow up but Tamar was forgotten. Next, we are told, Judah's wife died and now he was a widower. After a period of mourning, Judah returned to his business as the owner of large flocks of sheep. He planned a trip to Timnah to talk with his sheep shearers. When Tamar learned of this intended visit, she removed her widow's clothing, put on a veil and the clothes of a prostitute. She positioned herself at the entrance of her town which was on the road to Timnah. She knew where Judah would have to pass by.

As she intended, when Judah saw her, he assumed she was a prostitute. He turned aside to make a contract with her. They bargained for a price. It was agreed her payment for services rendered would be a kid from his flocks which would be sent to her the next day. Wise to the ways of the world, Tamar, still veiled, required Judah to give her something of value, something she would return when his payment of the lamb was received. They settled on Judah's signet ring as well as the cord wrapped around his waist and his staff. The two of them then went off to have their tryst. Afterward Judah went on his way. Tamar went back to her father's home and once more put on the garments of her widowhood.

The next day, Judah, true to his word, sent one of his servants with the lamb to redeem his property. This servant, however, could not find the woman. He inquired of the people of the village as to the identity of the prostitute who solicited business at the gates of this village. They claimed no one in their town had ever done that. The servant returned and reported to Judah his failure to locate this woman.

Judah, not willing to be the subject of ridicule, decided to forgo any further effort to recover his ring, cord and staff, charging them off as losses from a business deal. A number of months passed. Then Judah heard the local gossip that his daughter-in-law, Tamar, was pregnant and would soon produce a child by harlotry.

Judah was incensed at this news. Exercising his authority over this woman he had earlier rejected, he ordered her to be brought out and burned at the stake. As she was being led to her place of execution, she sent word to her father-in-law, saying, "I am with child by the man to whom these belong." She included his signet ring, his cord and his staff. Judah recognized them as his own and publicly repented. "She is more righteous than I, inasmuch as I did not give her to my son Shelah," he said. Because sex with one's daughter-in-law in that day was considered to be incest, Judah did not "lie with her again." (Gen. 38:26) He did provide for her care. After she gave birth, he married her and brought her into his harem. Tamar became the mother of twins whom she named Perez and Zerah.

Matthew, by using the name Tamar, incorporated her story into the genealogy of Jesus. Through this device he was saying the line that produced Jesus went through

Judah to Perez to the son of Perez, whose name was Hezron. Here, Matthew was asserting the Christ Child had an ancestor who was guilty of incest. It is certainly an interesting way to open a narrative about the Virgin Birth.

That, however, is only the first of the women Matthew alludes to in this genealogy. The other three are equally as fascinating and provocative. We will turn to each of them in detail as this story unfolds.

Rahab the Prostitute

The Second Woman in Matthew's Genealogy

The second woman mentioned in the genealogy of Matthew comes out of a story told in the book of Joshua. One can read the details in chapters two and six of that book. There are two noteworthy things about this woman. First, she is not a Jew. Rather she is a citizen of Jericho and thus presumably a Canaanite, i.e. a Gentile. Second, she is introduced and described in a single word, harlot. Rahab was a prostitute. She sold sex for gain.

Rahab had clearly entered the folk lore of both Judaism and Christianity. There are references to her in the Hebrew Scriptures in the book of Job: 9:13 and 26:12, in the Psalms: 87:4 and 89:10 and in the book of Isaiah 30:7 and 51:9. In addition to this reference in Matthew's genealogy, she is also referred to in the Christian Scriptures in two places, Hebrews 11:3 and James 2:35. It is difficult to establish any dependency between Matthew and these other New Testament references so we have to assume the story of Rahab must have been a popular one in both Judaism and in early Christianity. Following is a recounting of the narrative of Rahab as it appears in the book of Joshua.

The context is this: Moses has died in the wilderness of Moab. He has been buried by God acting alone in a mysterious and unknown grave. This is the story we find in the last chapter of Deuteronomy (34). Joshua, Moses' number one military captain, has assumed the position of the leader of these wandering, nomadic people. As if to validate Joshua with the authority of Moses, a crossing of the Jordan River in Red Sea fashion has been promised to Joshua. Beyond that river lay the first military prize for the invading Hebrews, the fortified and walled city of Jericho. While the people were encamped west of the Jordan preparing for the miraculous crossing, Joshua sent two men to spy on Jericho. These spies are unnamed, but they presumably managed to cross the river in daylight and enter the city, the gates of which were not closed until nightfall.

They immediately went, as if by some pre-arranged plan, to the house of Rahab the prostitute. Perhaps there was some kind of prior relationship. Perhaps they sought out this house, the only local brothel, for their own entertainment. Perhaps it made strategic sense. Rahab's house was conveniently located, built as it was into the wall encircling the city. A brothel might have been chosen simply to give the spies cover. We will never know.

There is also the probability this location and the services Rahab offered were well known to citizens and strangers alike. It was certainly in the public domain. Reality suggests that for a stranger to enter the city and go straight to the house of Rahab would arouse little suspicion. Whatever the reason or reasons, it was to Rahab's house that Joshua's spies went. There, the text says, they lodged. It seems they remained there for several days. In time, their presence became known. It would certainly arouse suspicion if regular customers were rebuffed because of the presence of these strangers. The public utterances of miffed regular customers would surely start rumors flying.

In any event, their presence quickly came to the attention of the authorities in Jericho including the king. Almost immediately they were defined as spies who had illegally entered the land. So the king, apparently knowing where

they were, sent a deputation of soldiers to the house of
Rahab with orders for the spies to come forth. Presumably
they were to be executed, the normal fate of spies.

Rahab, however, turns out to be more loyal to the spies
than she is to her city. When she gets wind of the danger,
she not only hides the spies, but she lies to the king's mes-
sengers about their continued presence. She did not deny
they had been there since that seemed to have been a well-
established fact. She admitted they had visited, but she
told them she had no idea where they were from or what
their business was in Jericho. They have now gone, she
said, telling the authorities the two men departed before
the gates of the city were closed when darkness fell.

What might have been her motive? Perhaps she was
just protecting her customers. Perhaps she had already developed a relationship with one of the spies that altered
her priorities. Whatever the reason, Rahab urged the king's
representatives to pursue these spies rapidly. Their depar-
ture from the city, she told them, had been recent and they
could surely be overtaken. All the while, according to this
narrative, Rahab had taken these men to the roof of her
house and hidden them under stalks of flax laid in order
on her roof.

The king's men took Rahab at her word and pursued
what they thought were the escaping spies to the Jordan
River and across it into the surrounding countryside.
When the pursuers left the city, the gates were closed for
the night. No one could now leave and the pursuers could
not return until dawn when the gates were reopened.

Rahab then goes to the roof to uncover her hidden
guests. She speaks to them as one who knows they are
destined to conquer Jericho. She tells them the fear of the
invading Hebrews had fallen upon her fellow citizens and
has caused their courage to melt away. She tells them the
people have heard of the miracle at the Red Sea and of

their conquest of the Amorites in the wilderness. The citizens of Jericho felt doomed.

Then she extracts an oath from the two spies. As I have protected you and dealt kindly with you, she said, I am prepared to continue to serve you by helping you escape. You must first, however, give me a sign that when your people conquer Jericho, you will repay my kindness by sparing my family from death. That means, she tells them, not just my life but those of my father, my mother, my brothers and sisters, their spouses and children. The spies agreed. "Our lives for your life and those of your extended family" was the deal. It seemed to them a fair bargain so it was agreed.

A sign was established. Rahab was to hang a scarlet cord in the window of her house in the protective wall. This cord would be seen by all who passed by. The spies swore that all who were gathered in this house with the scarlet cord would be spared. Then Rahab made a rope and lowered each of the spies in a basket to the ground outside the wall to safety. She instructed them to go to the hills through which their pursuers had already swept and hide there for three days until their pursuers had returned to the city.

Their escape was successful. After three days in the woods, they returned to Joshua with their report. The people of Jericho are faint hearted, the spies said. They know the Lord has given Jericho and its people into our hands.

Rahab then disappears from the drama until the conquest of Jericho occurs in chapter six. In the meantime, the swollen, flooded waters of the Jordan have been split in Red Sea-like fashion. The army of the Hebrews has crossed the river bed on dry land. They set up siege positions outside the walls of the city of Jericho.

For six days, the army walked around those walls following the Ark of the Lord's Covenant. They were attended by priests blowing constantly on their trumpets which were shofars or rams horns. On the seventh day, the Hebrew army walked around the city walls seven times, the ram's horns blowing constantly.

When the seventh journey around the walls was complete, the trumpets blew a long and sustained blast. The people shouted with loud shouts and, we are told, the walls around Jericho fell to the ground. Perhaps the sound vibrations from the shofars and the shouting people were more than their structures could tolerate. Perhaps the miraculous aspects of this story were enhanced with its telling as the years rolled by. The narrative was not written until some 300 years after the event was supposed to have taken place.

The important thing for our purpose is to note that this book says Joshua and his army destroyed Jericho. They put everyone to the edge of the sword—all men, all women, all old people, all young people and all the animals—in an act of genocidal fury. True to their word, however, they spared all those who gathered in the house of Rahab. Joshua gave specific orders, "Search out the harlot's house and bring out of it the woman and all who belong to her as we promised." The book of Joshua concludes the story by saying Rahab the harlot was saved and all her household "and she dwelt in Israel until this day."

From some source Matthew declared she married a man named Salmon. Was he one of the two spies? Once again, we will never know. But Matthew asserts that Salmon and Rahab had a baby boy whose name was Boaz. The line from Salmon went through Boaz to Obed, to Jesse and to David, who became the King of the Hebrew nation. This line would lead directly to Jesus of Nazareth who was of the house of David.

This is the second woman included in Matthew's genealogy of Jesus. The first was guilty of an incestuous relationship with her father-in-law, the second was a prostitute. Matthew is introducing the story of Jesus' birth. He is establishing the Jewish roots of Jesus as well as his royal roots. He was also stating in a loud and provocative way, the line that produced Jesus of Nazareth traveled through incest and harlotry. Why would he introduce the virgin birth this way? What was his agenda? What was his purpose? The story moves on and so does Matthew's genealogy. The third of these shady ladies in Matthew's genealogy next and she is a seductress.

The Role of Ruth

The Seductress

The third woman mentioned in Matthew's genealogy of Jesus is also unique in a number of ways. Her name is Ruth and she, like Rahab, is a foreigner. Rahab was a Canaanite citizen of Jericho. Ruth was a Moabite, the widow of a Jewish man named Mahlon. Her story is found in the tiny book bearing her name nestled in the Hebrew Scriptures between Judges and I Samuel. It is a dramatic tale involving some unfamiliar Jewish practices that are strange to us today. They made sense in terms of the Jewish values of the day, rooted as they were in both tribal and patriarchal assumptions. Listen first to the story.

It was around the year 1100 BCE when a time of famine produced a downturn in the Hebrew economy. Elimelech, a citizen of Bethlehem, his wife Naomi and their two sons, Mahlon and Chilion, moved to the land of Moab in search of work, food and survival. Soon thereafter, Elimelech died leaving Naomi with her two sons as strangers and aliens in a foreign land. The two sons assumed the care of their mother and settled into life in Moab, living there for about ten years. During that time they even took Moabite women to be their wives.

Mahlon married Ruth and Chilion married Orpah. Tragedy struck once again when both Mahlon and Chilion died. This left the remaining members a very vulnerable family of three widows, women who had no male support and no male protection. This patriarchal society had not developed any way of enabling lone women to care for themselves. Nothing was more frail or tragic in this society than a woman who had no father, no husband and no son. An independent woman was an unimaginable category.

Hebrew law required for women who are alone to be cared for by the nearest male kinsman in the family. Normally this meant the next oldest brother in the family must take the widow of his deceased brother as his wife. In the case of Naomi, Orpah and Ruth, however, there were no younger brothers. With Naomi being of post-menopausal age, there was no chance of ever producing any. She thus fell out of the social safety net meant to care for the vulnerable. The next level of support was to identify the male who was the closest of kin and to turn all of her assets over to him. This included his taking the widowed woman to be his wife, or at least a member of his harem, for which he had responsibility. He also assumed sexual privileges with the stated hope of raising up children to honor her deceased husband.

As long as this fragile trio of women lived in the land of Moab there was no male closest of kin. Naomi, facing this reality, called her two daughters-in-law to her and told them she was moving back to the land of the Jews, presumably to Bethlehem. She instructed the young widows to do the only thing left open to them. She told them to return to their families and to the protection of their fathers. This was a demeaning option as these widows would from then on be considered damaged goods. They would be unable to contract another proper marriage. Perhaps some men could be found to take them, but prospects were bleak. They were not as bleak, however, as what they faced as a family of three vulnerable women living alone. Orpah accepted that option and returned to her family, disappearing from this story forever.

Ruth, however, declined and informed Naomi she would go with her back to the land of the Jews. She did not want to leave her mother-in-law alone. Together they would face the hardships both knew awaited them.

In one of the most beautiful passages in this book, Ruth says words that have been set to music. Today we know them as *The Song of Ruth*. "Entreat me not to leave you or to return from following you; for where you go, I will go; where you lodge, I will lodge; your people shall be my people and your God shall be my God; where you die, I will die and there will I be buried." (Ruth 1:16–17) This song of Ruth is frequently sung at weddings as the bride and groom stare deeply into each other's eyes. I wonder how many couples would choose this music if they knew it was originally Ruth's song sung to her mother-in-law.

The two single women returned to Bethlehem and began their struggle for survival. It was the time of the beginning of the barley harvest. Naomi plotted her strategy. She was aware her husband, Elimelech, had a kinsman named Boaz, who owned much land in the Bethlehem area. She thus settled into a humble dwelling near the fields of her husband's distant relative. Jewish law also required the reapers should not seek to harvest every grain of barley. Some should be left in the field to be gleaned by the poor. Each day Ruth went into these fields to gather the grain the reapers had missed. She brought it home, ground it and baked it into a barley cake sufficient to keep Naomi and herself from starving.

Her faithful caring for Naomi was noticed. Boaz inquired of her identity and learned she was Naomi's Moabite daughter-in-law. She had asked permission to glean in the field behind the reapers, gathering the scanty remains from sunup to sundown without resting. Inspired by this example, Boaz spoke to Ruth, telling her not to gather grain in any other fields. He also gave her access to water drawn by the young men for the workers in the field. He ordered the young men not to molest her.

Ruth thanked Boaz for his kindness, inquiring as to why he was so gracious to a foreigner. Boaz replied that her faithfulness in the care of Naomi had inspired him. He revealed he had been told of the death of Ruth's husband and of her willingness to leave her own people in order to care for Naomi. Boaz then instructed the reapers to leave some of the sheaves they had gathered for her to glean. When Ruth told Naomi about the kindness of the man who owned the fields, Naomi was pleased. The trap she was setting was about to be sprung. She waited until the harvest season was over before she put her plan into operation.

Naomi shared with Ruth that Boaz was a distant relative of Elimelech, her father-in-law, and thus of Mahlon, Ruth's husband. Therefore he had a social responsibility to care for her. When the reaping was over, Boaz and his workers would celebrate at the threshing floor and Ruth would attend that celebration. She prepared carefully, bathing and anointing herself with perfume. She put on her best dress and off she went. Naomi instructed her that she was not to make herself known until Boaz had finished eating and drinking. The text says until "his heart was merry."

The wine flowed freely that evening and by midnight Boaz, now well drunk, lay down on the floor and went to sleep. Ruth came over to him, placed a pillow under his head and covered him with a blanket. Then the text says she uncovered his feet, and lay down at his feet. In the scriptures the word feet was a euphemism for the male genitals. The fact is, Ruth undressed him and climbed under the blanket with him. This was an overt act of seduction.

When Boaz awakened at the dawn's first shaft of light, he found this woman under the blanket with him. He had no idea who she was or what he might have done in his drunken stupor. "Who are you?" he asked her. She replied, "I am Ruth, you are my next of kin. Marry me." Boaz pretended to be flattered that she had not gone after a younger man, but he was not quite ready to accept this new responsibility. There was one other, he said, who was a closer kinsman to her husband. He would have to speak to him first. It seems this other man had the right of first refusal. Boaz went to meet with him, telling Ruth not to let it be known "that a woman came to the threshing floor." He then gave Ruth six measures of barley, perhaps as payment for her night's work, and he went off to the city. Ruth reported back to Naomi with this grain and Naomi rejoiced. Her plan had clearly worked.

Boaz, gathering ten men of the city to serve as witnesses, met with this nearest kinsman and the negotiations proceeded. Boaz informed this man that Ruth, Mahlon's widow, had returned from Moab. She has a parcel of land that belonged to Mahlon's father, our kinsman, Elimelech. You, as the nearest of kin, have first refusal. Will you redeem this land? If not, I am next in line.

The nearest of kin agreed to redeem it. Then Boaz said that is fine, but you need to know the day you take over this field, you are also agreeing to care for Naomi, Elimelech's widow. You must also take Mahlon's widow, Ruth, to be your wife and to raise up children to her deceased husband. That was a sticky wicket. He would then have to include any children he might have with Ruth among those who would inherit his estate. So he declined. "I cannot redeem it," he said, "Lest I impair my own children's inheritance." So, in the presence of the elders, he renounced his claim. The decision was affirmed in the traditional way by exchanging a sandal.

Thus Boaz was authorized to buy the parcel, to become heir of all that belonged to Elimelech, Mahlon and Chilion. He would care for Naomi and Ruth would become his wife so the name of Mahlon would not be cut off in the land. The elders saluted Boaz and said, "May your house be like the house of Perez, whom Tamar bore to Judah," thus linking these two stories. Boaz and Ruth had a son whose name was Obed. When Obed reached maturity, he had a son named Jesse. Jesse in turn grew up and had a son named David, who became the great king of the Hebrew nation. Ruth was thus the great grandmother of King David.

Matthew incorporated Ruth into the genealogy of Jesus which served as his prologue to the first account of Jesus' miraculous birth. In that genealogy, Matthew is claiming the line that produced Jesus of Nazareth flowed through the incest of Tamar, the harlotry of Rahab and the seduction of Ruth. It also proclaimed that Moabite blood flowed in the veins of the Jewish King David. This countered all the claims of racial purity made for the Royal House of David. One more woman will appear in Matthew's genealogy. We will turn to her story later. But surely by now we should be asking what Matthew's purpose was. What was the agenda he chose to introduce the Virgin Birth story in this way?

The Fourth Woman in Matthew's Genealogy

The Wife of Uriah

T he fourth and final woman included in Matthew's genealogy of Jesus with which he opens his gospel is the best known of them all. Simultaneously, he introduces into the Christian tradition the story of the virgin birth. In this genealogy, however, Matthew does not ever call her by her name. Rather he refers to her as the wife of Uriah. Those who are familiar with the Jewish scriptures, as Matthew's audience would surely have been, know from the story in the 11th chapter of II Samuel that her name is Bathsheba. You and I can read her fascinating story any time we want by turning to that chapter of the Bible. For those who might not be familiar with this narrative here are the details.

"In the spring of the year," is the way the author of this book of Samuel begins his story. The spring of the year is the time when the sap rises and romance is in the air. This author observes, it was also the time "when kings go forth to battle." King David, however, did not follow the familiar script for this year. He remained in Jerusalem while dispatching his army into battle under the command of Joab, his trusted military chief. Joab's assigned task, said the author of II Samuel, was to ravage King David's enemy, the Ammonites. Not only was he to conquer the land of Ammon, but his army was to accomplish this by besieging and then destroying the capitol city of Rabbah.

Meanwhile, the king remained safe and secure in the comfort of his palace.

Thus the stage was set in which this particular episode would transpire. While the king was at home, far from the battlefield, he would have the adventure that would determine not just the history of the Jewish people, but also through them, the history of the world. Great changes do attach themselves sometimes to seemingly unimportant details.

Late in the afternoon one day, King David, perhaps bored, decided to stroll out onto the rooftop of the royal palace to enjoy the warm spring breezes. Because his palace was the tallest building in the city, he could look down on all the roof tops of the other homes below. On this day, to the delight of his lecherous eyes, his gaze fell upon a young woman who was bathing herself in what she believed was the privacy of her own roof top. David was immediately smitten by this woman's charms. As heads of state are prone to do, he assumed his desires should be fulfilled. After inquiring as to her identity, David sent a messenger to this woman's house bearing his personal invitation for her to come to the palace to have a tryst with the king. She came. Whether or not she had a choice, we do not know. The rights of women were very restricted in that patriarchal society.

Bathsheba's roof top sunbath was described in this text as necessary for "purifying herself from her uncleanness." This was the euphemistic way the Bible explained she had just completed her menstrual cycle. This detail is essential to the developing plot of this story. It demonstrated conclusively she was not pregnant at that moment. When she arrived at the palace David greeted her and then "took her and lay with her." The act complete, this woman, having served her defined purpose, returned to her own house. In all probability David thought little more about the incident. It was probably not the first time, nor would it be the last, this kind of activity had happened in his life. It was, however, destined to be a life-changing experience in Bathsheba's life.

In a few weeks Bathsheba, noticing some revealing circumstances, sent a message to the palace marked for the king's eyes only. In this message she informed King David she was pregnant with his child. David, seeking to create some room in which to maneuver, asked her how she could be sure this baby was his child. "You are a married woman," he reminded her. "Why do you assume this is not your husband's child?"

Bathsheba informed him that though she was indeed married, her husband, Uriah, was a professional soldier. He had been away for months serving in the king's army under Captain Joab in the war against the Ammonites. "There is no way, oh King," she concluded, "that you are not the father of this baby."

David felt the noose tightening around his neck. However, he was not ready to take responsibility for this situation so he opted for plan B. He dispatched a messenger to Joab, his military army chief, ordering him to grant a furlough to Uriah the Hittite. His cover was that he wanted to receive a first-hand report from someone in the field of battle and he had chosen Uriah for this signal honor. While on this special leave, David reasoned, Uriah would stay in his home and lie with his wife. When the baby was born, they could claim the infant had just come early. It would not be the first time in those pre-DNA times that such an explanation had been successfully employed.

So a very surprised Uriah received orders to return to Jerusalem in order to provide a personal and private update for the king on the course of the battle. Uriah, however, did not choose to return to his own house. He slept quite ostentatiously in the street at the gate of the king's palace. David's plans were foiled again. He had not counted on Uriah being the ultimate Boy Scout. Uriah told the king it would simply not be fitting for him to enjoy the pleasures of his home, his wife and his bed while his comrades were still camping out in the fields, eating K-rations and risking their lives in the siege of Rabbah. "I could not think of doing such a thing," he concluded. David must have thought to himself, "What a turkey!" Now he was forced to resort to plan C.

The king next took out the royal quill and on a piece of royal parchment, he wrote out new orders to be carried to Joab, his military captain. He sent these new orders to Captain Joab via the hand of Uriah who was returning to his duty on the battlefield. The king's orders directed Joab to charge the gates of the city of Rabbah with a V shaped flying wedge. These orders also directed Joab to place Uriah the Hittite at the point of the V thus giving him the honor of leading the charge. It was a position in which few survived.

It was done as the king commanded and Uriah was struck down and killed immediately. Joab then sent the king a message to inform him his problems were over. Uriah was dead. In turn, David sent for Bathsheba and she came to his palace to be one of his wives and thus a member of his harem.

Bathsheba turned out to be a wife who exercised considerable power. The child of her adulterous liaison with the king died in infancy. Solomon, Bathsheba's second son by King David, was destined to succeed King David at his death. This was in spite of the fact he was not close to being the first-born son and thus the presumed heir to the throne. With the assistance of a priest named Zadok, a military leader named Benaiah, and a prophet named Nathan, Bathsheba maneuvered to secure the throne for her son. King Solomon in turn secured the power of the royal family. He was destined to rule the people of Judah for over 400 years. That is Bathsheba's story as found in the Bible.

In his genealogy, Matthew traces the royal line from Solomon through the kings of Judah until the royal family was destroyed by the Babylonians in the period of history called the Exile. Then he picks up the genealogy and traces it from the Exile to a man named Joseph. The conclusion of his genealogy says "Jacob was the father of Joseph, the husband of Mary, of whom Jesus is born, who is called Christ." Thus the genealogy, with which Matthew opened his gospel and which served to introduce the story of Jesus' supernatural or virgin birth, is brought to a conclusion.

As we come to the end of this opening genealogy ask yourself, what was Matthew's purpose in beginning his gospel in this way? Why did he deem it necessary and appropriate to say the line that produced Jesus of Nazareth began with Abraham and traveled through the royal family, into the exile and concludes at the life on which the whole story is to focus? Finally, what is he trying to communicate when he places into the background of Jesus, four well-known women in Jewish history? All of them, by the standards of that day, were sexually compromised women. At the very opening of his story, the line that produced Jesus of Nazareth flowed through the incest of Tamar (Gen. 38), the prostitution of Rahab (Joshua 2, 6), the seduction of Ruth (Ruth 3) and the adultery of Bathsheba (II Samuel 11). That appears to be what the text of Matthew's gospel reveals.

Perhaps that accounts, at least in part, for the fact that throughout most of Christian history, the first 17 verses of Matthew's first chapter were skipped and ignored. They were called the most boring verses in the Bible, the who-begat-whoms. No one was encouraged to look at them or take them seriously. Perhaps this strange introduction reveals there is far more to the story of the virgin birth than we have imagined in the past.

We will continue to look at Matthew's birth narrative. Then we will turn to Luke's account of Jesus' birth. Studying the Bible can be quite exciting once one removes the blinders of literalism and begins to look at the texts for what they are. So stay tuned. We will move next to Matthew's proof text found in Isaiah 7:14 and then to the wise men and their familiar gifts. It is a fascinating study. I hope you are finding it so.

Was There Scandal at the Manger?

T he prologue to Mathew's gospel, which also serves to introduce the story of Jesus' miraculous birth, is now complete. Matthew, writing to the members of a traditional Jewish community who were also the followers of Jesus, has grounded the life of Jesus deeply into Jewish history. Jesus is the son of Abraham, the heir of King David, in a line produced by those who had lived the various periods of Jewish life. The Jews were a people who had been born free in the persons of the great patriarchs.

Driven by famine into the land of Egypt they descended into slavery but broke free once more in the Exodus. Wandering through the wilderness they reclaimed what they believed was their promised land. They established a lasting monarchy but were torn by secession and civil wars. Defeated in battle at the hands of the Babylonians they were once more exiled to a foreign land where they believed the songs of Zion could never be sung again. Years later, they were finally allowed to return to their homeland. They rebuilt their ruins, including their holy city of Jerusalem, and revived their ancient calling to be a blessing to the nations of the world. These were the people who produced Jesus, Matthew was saying. Matthew believed the hope of the Jews was vested in this life of Jesus.

In his stage-setting genealogy, however, Matthew had also begun to respond to the critics of Jesus. At this time they were primarily identified with the Orthodox party of the Jewish world. What was the content of their attack on Jesus? I think we find hints of it in various places in the New Testament. I will turn to them when we have stitched together the content of this criticism. Then I believe we will discover Matthew's motive for developing the story of Jesus' origins in the way he did. Most especially we will be able to understand just why Matthew included in his genealogy the references to those women I have called the shady ladies. He demonstrated the line that produced Jesus also flowed through incest, prostitution, seduction and adultery.

Religion has always been in the business of control. This is why those who cannot abide by its rules face ostracism and excommunication. The religious lines of power are clear. God reveals the divine law to the religious leaders. These religious leaders then claim for themselves alone the power to interpret and to enforce those rules. To disobey the rules is not just to disobey the religious leaders, but it is also to disobey the God who has chosen and empowered these leaders.   A religious trouble-maker is, therefore, the most direct threat to ecclesiastical power. Religious reformers and religious visionaries are thus thought of as dangerous people. They challenge the security around which the religious community is organized. That is why reformers are banished, tortured and executed, sometimes by being burned at the stake. Prior to this final solution, visionaries are frequently attacked personally, becoming the victims of character assassination. One of the ways this character assassination was accomplished in Jewish society in the first century was to attack the reformer or the visionary's legitimacy. A base-born person might be prone, they assumed, to struggle against the religious rules that defined him or her as untrustworthy.

That is why there is so much discussion in the gospel tradition about the origins of Jesus. He was not thought of by the religious hierarchy as a legitimate religious leader. He came from Galilee. Search the scriptures. Nowhere will you find a hint that a messiah would rise from Galilee. He hailed from the town of Nazareth. That was on the wrong side of the tracks. Nothing good could come out of Nazareth. Where did this man get his knowledge, his power? We know his family, his mother, his brothers and his sisters. Echoes of his inadequate origins are found throughout the gospel tradition. Some even suggested he might be possessed by demons. By the power of Beelzebub, he casts out demons, is the way they put it.

Mark, the earliest gospel to be written, makes these charges overt. In chapter three of that first gospel, in which there is no birth story, the family of Jesus is portrayed as becoming alarmed at the reputation Jesus was accumulating. Believing him to be beside himself, that is, out of his mind, his mother and his brothers actually come to take him away. They are rebuked by Jesus. He declares his real family, his real mother and siblings, are not his birth and blood relatives but those who hear the word of God and obey it.

By the time one arrives at chapter six of Mark, these charges have finally been identified with Jesus' questionable paternity. A member of the crowd shouts, "Is not this the carpenter?" Note that Joseph has never been mentioned. Jesus is the carpenter in the first gospel to be written. This nameless voice in the crowd goes on with this identification process and says, "Is not this the son of Mary, the mother of James and Joses and Judas and Simon and are not his sisters here with us?" Then Mark says, "They took offense at him."

Three things must be noted here. First, to call an adult Jewish male the son of his mother was a deliberate insult. It carries with it the implication that his paternity is unknown. His father is compromised, missing or not identified. It is a charge of being illegitimate. Secondly, this is the only time the mother of Jesus is identified by the name Mary in any Christian writing before the ninth decade. The final thing to note is in this, the earliest record we have about the family of Jesus, no father—earthly or otherwise—is mentioned. Joseph does not enter the Christian story until we get to Matthew in the ninth decade. When he is introduced, his role is to name the child and thus to legitimize him.

Another hint of Jesus' questionable paternity is found in the Song of Mary, called *The Magnificat*, recorded only by Luke. In that song, God is said "to have regarded the low estate of his handmaiden" and to have turned her to a state of blessedness. God exalted her, who was of low degree. There was no status of lower degree or lower estate in first century Jewish society than an unmarried woman expecting a child.

A third scriptural hint that rumors were abroad about Jesus' questionable paternity is found in the Fourth Gospel. Once again, the subject is the inadequate origins of Jesus that disqualify him from being able to make the messianic claim clearly being made for him. In this passage someone in the crowd shouts at Jesus, "We were not born of fornication." (John 8:41). This speaker's clear presumption is that Jesus was.

Jesus' origins were under attack with innuendos abroad that he was base-born, a bastard, if you will. This is what actually caused him to be a troublemaker. Matthew decides to come to his defense. He will argue that far from being base-born, his life was born holy. God is his father. Borrowing a popular Mediterranean tradition which attributed personal greatness to divine origins and virgin births, Matthew created the narrative of Jesus' miraculous birth. He then searched the scriptures to find a prophetic text that might point in this direction. He found a verse in

Isaiah (7:14). It did not fit but, like many fundamentalists today, Matthew edited it to make it fit. The text literally said in Hebrew, a young woman is with child. Translated into Greek, the Hebrew word for woman, almah, was rendered parthenos in which there is a connotation of virginity. However, the phrase "a virgin is with child" is an oxymoron, so Matthew altered the verse to read: "a virgin will conceive." On the basis of this forced and incorrect rendition of this text, Matthew built the first story of the virgin birth of Jesus to appear in Christian history.

The text in Isaiah actually grew out of a time in the 8th century BCE when the city of Jerusalem was under siege by the combined armies of Syria and the Northern Kingdom. The prophet Isaiah wanted to provide a sign to assure Judah's King, Ahaz, that Jerusalem would not fall to these enemies and the Jewish nation would go on. His reference was to the current pregnancy of a woman in the royal family, probably the daughter-in-law of King Ahaz. The birth of her royal child would be a sign that the nation would endure and thus the House of David would not be destroyed. His re-assuring words were: "A woman is with child." The context makes it obvious this verse did not apply to someone who would be born 750 years later.

Matthew, as a follower of Jesus, was convinced of the holiness of Jesus' life and the reality of his experience that God was in and with Jesus in a deep and dramatic way. So he crafted the virgin birth story to support that thesis. Matthew, however, must have known his reasoning was weak. He was enough of a student of the Hebrew Scriptures to know the text he had chosen would not bear the weight he had assigned to it. So, in the prologue, he covered his other bases. This life is holy. This life is of God. This life is God's promised messiah. If you are not persuaded by my argument from scripture, I want you to know that whatever were the circumstances surrounding his birth, God is capable of bringing holiness through any set of human compromises. Out of a line that contained incest, prostitution, seduction and adultery, this holy life of God has emerged. Thus it is a powerful story.

Matthew will continue to wrap the Jewish scriptures around Jesus for the rest of his birth narrative. As he does so, the history of the Jewish people and the characters out of that ancient Jewish story re-emerge to bear their witness. Those who possess Jewish eyes will be able to see them. Among these characters will be Moses, the Pharaoh, Joseph the patriarch, Rachel, Isaiah, the Queen of Sheba, Balaam, Balak, Jesse, David, Hosea, Elijah and Joshua. Matthew's gospel in general, but the birth narrative in particular, must be read through a Jewish lens. We will turn to these other texts and biblical characters as we continue the journey.

Matthew Sources and the Hebrew Scriptures

R eading the Bible with any real comprehension in the 21st century is not an easy task. The gospels are a product of the first century, a dramatically different time. They reflect a vastly different culture. They do not translate easily. Most Christians do not realize Christianity itself was born in the womb of first-century Judaism and it did not leave that womb until some 50 to 60 years after the crucifixion of Jesus. To say it another way, the Christian movement did not separate itself from the synagogue until late in the ninth decade of the Christian era. This means the gospels of Mark, Matthew and probably Luke were all written while Christianity was still a movement within the synagogue. Only John, the last gospel to be written, reflects a time after the synagogue and the church had separated.

While the disciples of Jesus were still members of the synagogue they would have listened to the Hebrew Scriptures being read each and every Sabbath. They would have searched within them for what they were certain were messianic clue. They believed this would help them process and understand their experience with Jesus of Nazareth. That is, they looked to the Hebrew Scriptures to enable them to understand both his meaning and his appeal. The gospels reflected the fact that they had wrapped the memory of Jesus inside their understanding of these Scriptures. As fellow members of the synagogue, they knew the stories of their Jewish past. They would recognize when part of that tradition was being used first in preaching and later in gospel writing to illuminate the Jesus experience.

By the middle years of the second century of the Christian era, however, the followers of Jesus had become almost exclusively a Gentile movement. This meant the Jewish knowledge necessary to understand the gospels, which were products of the synagogue, had no relevance among the Gentile faithful. So it was that these Gentile Christians began to manifest profoundly ignorant attitudes toward the gospels. This resulted in both a tendency toward literalization and a heightened sense of the supernatural and the miraculous. That distortion plagues the Christian Church to this day. These ideas, almost unknown among Jewish worshipers, became quite popular in Gentile Christian circles. This is despite the fact that they badly distorted the relationship of the story of Jesus to the Hebrew Scriptures and especially to the writings of the prophets.

Among the disciples of Jesus the historical reality is that the process was the other way around. Convinced as these followers were that Jesus was the promised messiah, they pored over the messianic expectations permeating Jewish biblical thinking. This was especially true after the time of the Babylonian exile in the first quarter of sixth century BCE. Then they forced their memories of Jesus to conform to what they determined were scriptural prophetic expectations. Thus the Servant passages of II Isaiah (Is. 40–55) shaped many aspects of the first written version of the story of the cross. In the process, Jesus was obliged to look more and more like Isaiah's Servant. The Shepherd King of II Zechariah (9–14) was also a determinative figure. The Shepherd King came riding to his people on a donkey. Then he was removed for 30 pieces of silver by those who bought and sold animals in the Temple. This is a good illustration of how the process worked.

In addition, narratives from the lives of the great figures of Jewish history were regularly magnified and then retold about Jesus of Nazareth. When we read the gospels, we should not be surprised to discover events that occurred in the lives of former Jewish heroes. People like Moses, Samuel, Elijah and Elisha among others, were simply retrofitted by the gospel writers and then retold as if they had happened in the life of Jesus of Nazareth.

Matthew employed this technique over and over again in his story of Jesus' birth. Everything Matthew related as happening to Jesus during his infancy was in fact designed to place his life into what Matthew believed were the messianic expectations chronicled in the Hebrew Scriptures.

Matthew was also writing apologetically. That is, he was seeking to defend Jesus and the Jesus movement against charges being leveled against them. First there was what came to be called the scandal of the cross. Jesus was crucified, a fact that seemed to violate all messianic expectations. The passion stories in both Paul and the gospels speak to this issue. When critics in the 9th decade of the Common Era began to question Jesus' paternity, something that might be called the scandal of the crib arose. Matthew, who was the first author to introduce a narrative about the birth of Jesus, responded directly to those charges.

We need to be aware, as Matthew surely was, of the deep, historic division in Jewish history between the tribe of Judah and the ten other tribes, who came to be called the Northern Kingdom of Israel. Judah was ruled by the House of David. The Northern Kingdom never established a long term ruling family. They identified its people as the descendants of Joseph, the favorite son of the patriarch Jacob. After wrestling with an angel, Jacob had his name changed to Israel. If Jesus was truly to be messiah, his first task was to bring together the Judah traditions in Hebrew history with the Joseph traditions of Hebrew history.

Matthew did this first in the genealogy by going from Abraham through Judah to David and Solomon. He then proceeded through the royal house of David, which ruled Judah from 1000 BCE to 586 BCE. The Judah root of Jesus' life was thus clear. Next he introduced into his story an earthly father, whose role it was to protect and to legitimize Jesus and gave to him the name Joseph. To make his readers certain of his purpose, he then developed the biographical details of this Joseph character right out of the Hebrew Scriptures.

Please be aware that no father of Jesus was ever been mentioned anywhere prior to the writing of Matthew. There are no references to Joseph in any of the epistles of Paul (CE 51–64) and none in Mark, the first gospel to be written (CE 70–72). There are some who argue that both the Q document and the Gospel of Thomas also antedate Mark. I do not agree with that, but even if they were proved to be true, there is no reference to Joseph in either of those sources.

Matthew appears to be the one who chose the name of Joseph for the character he would create as the earthly father of Jesus. This Joseph was then assigned a primary role in Matthew's story of the virgin birth. In that patriarchal society, someone had to be the guardian of this vulnerable, pregnant woman and eventually of her infant and presumed illegitimate, son. Matthew made those the duties of Joseph. Once this character became part of his story, Matthew then had to flesh out his creation with content. It should come as no surprise he would draw that content from the story of the patriarch Joseph in Genesis (37–50).

In this Genesis story, one discovers three primary identifiers associated with the patriarch Joseph. First, he has a father named Jacob. Second, he is associated again and again with dreams. In the Genesis story, the young Joseph is always dreaming about how important he will become. In his adult life, while in prison, he becomes the interpreter of the dreams of two people hauled into prison by the Pharaoh. One was the Pharaoh's butler and the other was the Pharaoh's baker. Joseph's interpretations of these two men's dreams come true. Then he becomes the interpreter of the Pharaoh's dreams. He rides on this ability into political power in Egypt. The Genesis patriarch, Joseph, is overwhelmingly identified with dreams.

Third this Joseph is also given the task in Jewish history of saving the people of the covenant from death. This threat of death to the Hebrew people came in the form of a famine in which starvation was real. How did Joseph save them? He took them down into the land of Egypt where food was still plentiful.

Now look closely at the character of Joseph as drawn by Matthew in the birth narrative which opens his story of Jesus. Matthew makes three claims for this Joseph. First, he tells us Joseph had a father named Jacob. Second, Matthew portrays his Joseph, just like the patriarch Joseph, as being constantly associated with dreams. God never speaks to him except through a dream. In a dream God, or the angel of the Lord, instructs Joseph to take Mary to himself assuring him the child she is having is of the Holy Spirit. In a dream, Joseph is instructed to flee from death at the hands of Herod. In a dream, Joseph is directed to return to their Bethlehem home following the death of Herod. Then in a dream, Joseph is told to seek the safety of a town in Galilee called Nazareth so the child might grow up in relative security. Finally, just as the role of Joseph in the book of Genesis was to save the people of the covenant from death by fleeing to Egypt, so now Matthew's Joseph will save the messianic figure of Jesus from death by fleeing with him to Egypt.

This is not literal history. Joseph is a literary creation, not a person of history. The flight to Egypt was a literary device to link Jesus to Moses. This Joseph then disappears from the biblical story as soon as the birth narratives are complete and is never portrayed again in any context. Jewish readers would recognize Matthew's sources. Later Gentile readers would not. Because they did not understand, they would assume they were reading history.

At every point in Matthew's story, the symbols, drawn out of the Hebrew Scriptures, are not just present, but they have been incorporated into the memory of Jesus. We will examine those quoted passages from Isaiah, Micah, Jeremiah, Hosea and a final mysterious source. Matthew's message is clear. He has interpreted Jesus as the fulfillment of the expectations found in the Jewish Scriptures.

Matthew Weaves Together Proof Texts from Isaiah, Micah, Hosea and from an Unknown Source

C hristianity was born in the synagogue and the original followers of Jesus were primarily observant Jews. They regularly gathered for worship in the synagogue on the Sabbath. A major part of that worship consisted of reading, learning about and becoming conversant with the sacred scriptures as the Jews understood them. Each Sabbath three major scripture readings were observed by the synagogue. This was the traditional pattern of Jewish worship.

The first, the longest and the most important, came from what the Jews called the Torah. This part of the Hebrew Bible was also called *The Books of Moses*. In Jesus' day, it was generally believed Moses was the author of the Torah books; Genesis, Exodus, Leviticus, Numbers and Deuteronomy. These writings were the Jewish Holy of Holies. The stricter, more orthodox synagogues, required the entire Torah to be read in the synagogue on the Sabbaths in a single year. To accomplish this, the Torah lesson would of necessity consist of the reading of five to six chapters of our present text as the first lesson. It would take a minimum of 10 to 15 minutes to read a passage of that length. In more moderate or liberal synagogues this requirement was loosened and the Torah was allowed to be read over a three-year cycle.

The second lesson would come from the portion of the Hebrew Bible the Jews called *The Former Prophets.* These books purport to describe Jewish history after the death of Moses. It includes those works known as Joshua, Judges, I and II Samuel and I and II Kings. At an earlier point in history, these latter four books were all called the books of Samuel or I, II, III and IV Samuel. It was a later interpolation to call the last two I and II Kings. These books covered Jewish history from the conquest of Canaan under Joshua, around the year 1200 BCE, to the defeat of the nation of Judah at the hands of the Babylonians. The subsequent exile of the Jewish people to the land of Babylon began in 586 BCE. They were not as important as the Torah so there was no specific deadline by which to complete them.

The third synagogue scripture reading was from what the Jews called *The Latter Prophets.* That title referred to the books we now call Isaiah, Jeremiah, Ezekiel and the books from Hosea to Malachi. They were all on a single scroll and were referred to by the Jews as *The Book of the Twelve.* Christians tend to call them *The Minor Prophets.* Please note, Daniel did not come into the canon of Jewish Scripture until about 165 BCE. As a late arrival, it was not generally included in synagogue readings. Isaiah, Jeremiah, Ezekiel and *The Book of the Twelve* are about the same length and each tended to be read one chapter a week, one book a year. These four books would be rotated over a four-year cycle. The singing or reciting of selected psalms would break up and separate the various scripture readings.

Following these three readings, the members of the congregation would be invited to comment on the readings. The followers of Jesus began to wrap their memories of Jesus around and into the stories from the sacred text of the Jews. In time, stories originally written about Moses or Elijah would be retrofitted and then retold about Jesus.

This linked him to the spiritual power of his Jewish ancestors.

On other occasions, words from one of the prophets or from one of the psalms would illuminate an experience they once had with Jesus. A tradition started in which Jesus and the Hebrew Scriptures began to meld into each other. We will see this reality occurring over and over as we work through the gospels. For now, all I want to demonstrate is that these themes are a major part of the birth narratives and we cannot read them intelligently unless we recognize the process that created them.

We have already noted that the story of a wicked king or Pharaoh, who tried to put to death the infant Moses as God's promised deliverer, was repackaged and told by Matthew as a Jesus story. Consequently, a wicked king named Herod tries to put to death God's promised deliverer named Jesus. Matthew goes on to wrap his narrative of Jesus around a series of carefully chosen texts suggesting the history of the Jewish people is somehow being relived through Jesus. Thus the words of the Hebrew Scriptures find their fulfillment in him. Matthew is much like a country preacher trying to bend the biblical text to the needs of his sermon. In his birth story, Matthew borrows texts from Isaiah, Micah, Jeremiah, Hosea and, finally, from an unknown or yet to be identified text. I will examine each in brief detail. All of them are, at the very least, enormous stretches in literal accuracy.

The first one is Isaiah 7:14 which we have heard numerous times in our Christmas pageants. Out of the darkness or even off stage, the voice of the prophet is heard saying, "Behold, a virgin shall conceive and bear a son and his name shall be called Emmanuel, which means God with us." The first major problem with Matthew's use of this text is that he did not quote it accurately. Was this an honest mistake or a deliberate attempt to make the text say what he needed it to say to suit his literary purposes? No one can conclusively say, but I suspect the latter when I put these words from Isaiah into their original context. Isaiah actually writes in Hebrew, "Behold a young woman is with child." It is rather difficult to claim one is a virgin when one is expecting a baby. Indeed, the word virgin appears nowhere in this verse from Isaiah.

The context is this. Two kings, Pekah from the Northern Kingdom called Israel, and Rezin, the king of Syria, are in siege positions outside the walls of Jerusalem. They have made war on Judah and its king named Ahaz because he has refused to join their alliance against Assyria. Their goal in this war was to topple Ahaz and put a puppet king on the throne of Judah. Then Judah's military strength would be added to their alliance designed to hold off the Assyrians.

King Ahaz is atop the walls of Jerusalem inspecting its defenses when he is met by Isaiah the prophet. First, Isaiah assures the king that Jerusalem will not fall to "these smoldering stumps," which is what he calls Pekah and Rezin. Ahaz is not convinced. Isaiah then says to him: "Ask for a sign of God." He tells him God will convince you that you will be delivered. Ahaz refuses to ask.
Irritated, Isaiah says you will be given a sign whether you like it or not. "Behold a woman is with child." This baby, soon to be born into the royal household, will be the heir to the throne, a sign this kingdom will endure. Before this baby, is able to eat curds and honey and before he is old enough to choose between good and evil, these kings before whom Ahaz was quaking, will be long gone. The facts of history are this. The land of Judah was destined to work out a treaty with Assyria that left Judah a vassal state, but still alive. Both Syria and the Northern Kingdom of Israel were destroyed by Assyria. This text in Isaiah had nothing to do with predicting the birth of the messiah almost 800

years later. Matthew was stretching his interpretive powers wildly by using the text the way he did.

The second text from the prophets, which Matthew weaves into his story, comes from Micah. The wise men, described later in this narrative, stop to ask directions at the palace of King Herod. The king consults his chief priests and scribes to determine where the messiah is to be born.

One important image for the Jews was that the messiah must be a descendant of King David and thus heir to the Jewish throne. Part of the messiah's task was to restore the throne of King David. Micah the prophet refers to Bethlehem as the town out of which David emerged to rule the land of the Jews. Therefore, the messiah must follow the same pattern. So in the opening narratives of Matthew, the birth of Jesus was shifted from Nazareth, where he was surely born, to Bethlehem. Thus the messianic claim can be made and the words of the prophet Micah affirmed.

Next, Matthew proceeds to tell the story of King Herod slaughtering the boy babies in Bethlehem in his effort to destroy the promised deliverer. He relates this to another tragic moment in Jewish history when the Assyrians conquered and destroyed the Northern Kingdom. According to tradition, the Northern Kingdom was primarily made up of the descendants of Joseph, the son of Rachel, who was said to have been Jacob's favorite wife. Thus Jeremiah portrays Rachel, the tribal mother of the Northern Kingdom, as weeping for her children who are now lost forever. Matthew sees in that story a prediction of the deaths of the children at Herod's hand. It was not even a close fit.

Then Matthew says that when Joseph was forced to flee from Herod's wrath, he took Mary and the Christ Child to Egypt. Previously, God called the Jewish people out of Egypt. Now Matthew quotes Hosea, who was referring to Moses and the Exodus, and parlays it into the time when

Mary and the Christ Child were also called out of Egypt. The messiah, you see, must relive the history of the Jews.

In Matthew's final birth narrative, Joseph took Mary and the Christ Child to live in Nazareth. This, Matthew said, was to fulfill the words of the prophet that "he will be called a Nazarene." Such a prophetic expectation cannot be found anywhere in scripture. The closest we can come to it is in Isaiah 11:1 where the prophet writes "There shall come forth a shoot from the stump of Jesse (David's father) and a branch shall grow out of his roots." It is another text used to prove the messiah must be related to David. The word branch in Hebrew is nazir or nezer. It sounds a bit like Nazareth, but close is all Matthew needed. Matthew stretched all of his texts, but this last one was stretched to absolute fantasy.

My point is to show how the debate waged in the synagogue as the followers of Jesus sought to understand him, his relationship to the concept of messiah and his relationship to the Jewish Scriptures. We are reading here a first century Jewish interpretation of Jesus. We are not reading history. There is a difference.

Making Sense of the Wise Men

Having described the miraculous birth of Jesus in chapter one of his gospel, Matthew turns to his account of how the birth of Jesus was divinely rolled out to bring it to the attention of all the people of the world. His vehicle for this is to tell us a story of magi who follow a star moving across the sky. This star, they are purported to believe, will lead these wise men to discover the meaning Matthew has found contained in the life of this Jesus. Was this narrative the product of someone's historical memory? Of course not. That is never the source of powerful interpretive legends. Matthew went to the Hebrew Scriptures, his traditional source for material, in order to tell his story of Jesus. In those scriptures he found all the elements he needed to weave together the familiar narrative we now know as the story of the three wise men. Following Matthew's example, I invite you to come with me to look deeply into these Hebrew Scriptures.

First, let me direct your attention to a passage in Isaiah 60. It calls to its readers to "Arise, shine, for your light has come." The point Matthew was seeking to make in the entirety of his gospel was that in Jesus of Nazareth, the light which was destined to interrupt this world's darkness, had in fact arrived. Please note the universal quality of the star which serves as his symbol of this light. A star is visible to all the people of the world. A star is trans-national and it has the mystical power, he believes, to draw all nations toward its light.

Following a star is a familiar mythological reference to seeking the fulfillment of one's dreams. The birth of Jesus was precisely this for Matthew. The light of God dawned in the darkness of the entire world. Kings, Isaiah asserts, will therefore "come to the brightness of your rising." In Matthew's creative mind, the wise men begin to emerge out of the shadows as he is inspired by this passage. Isaiah goes on to say that these kings will come on camels. Then he says they will come from Sheba and guess what they will bring? Gold and frankincense, says Isaiah. Does that not begin to sound just a little bit familiar?

There are always among us, however, those who are religious literalists. So inevitably they will ask, "But where is the myrrh?" To get only two out of three gifts of the wise men from this text hardly makes a conclusive case. However, let me take you back to this text from Isaiah (60:1–6) and ask you to read it again, this time even more carefully. The Isaiah narrative states, "Those from Sheba will come." Sheba? Can you not hear the Jewish minds seeking connections by ranging over the entirety of their Jewish history? Matthew is telling us of kings "who will come to the brightness of God's rising." He is certain this will occur in the land of the Jews, which deserves, he believes, the homage of the world.

He is proclaiming Jesus to be that new king of the Jews. The word Sheba in the text immediately reminds him of another celebrated occasion in Jewish history. At that time another royal visitor came to pay homage to another king of the Jews. So, back into his memory of the scriptures he goes until he brings forth the story of the Queen of Sheba visiting King Solomon (I Kings 10:1–13).

Reading that story he discovers this queen also comes on camels, bearing gifts. The author of II Kings tells us these gifts consisted of gold, precious stones and spices. That text emphasizes the spices. It was, the text says, "an abundance of spices." The Queen of Sheba brought wagonloads of them, to be specific.

The only spice familiar to the people of the Middle East at this time was myrrh, a sweet smelling resin derived from a bush. The Jewish people used it first as a deodorant. Cleanliness and personal hygiene were in short supply in that day. Myrrh tempered body odors. Secondly myrrh came to be used as the spice of death. The Jews did not embalm their dead. They simply wrapped the deceased body in a cloth or shroud and then filled the shroud with sweet smelling myrrh to mask the odors of death and decay. Burial was not postponed for very long in that time and place.

So, out of the Hebrew Scriptures, Matthew discovers a text in which a light shining in the darkness attracts kings on camels to come to that light. These kings bring gifts of gold, frankincense and myrrh. The essential elements of the story of the wise men are thus found in the Jewish Scriptures.

The three gifts Matthew has the wise men bring to the Christ child were also symbols used by this gospel writer to introduce the adult Jesus to his readers. Gold was a gift appropriate to offer a king. "Born a king on Bethlehem's plain," says hymn writer John Henry Hopkins (1820–1891). More than anyone else, Hopkins put the story of the wise men into the life of our culture. He wrote *We Three Kings of Orient Are,* a hymn known and loved by all. Because Jesus was perceived as a king, the hymn continues by having one of the wise men say: "Gold I bring to crown him again." Matthew was thus introducing Jesus at the beginning of his gospel as the expected messianic king who was heir to the throne of David. He was destined to be born in David's city of Bethlehem to a virgin and her betrothed.

There were no birth records he could have searched for corroboration. This is not researched history; this is a Jewish interpretive legend. Matthew's original readers would surely have understood that fact.

Frankincense was thought of as a gift to be offered to a deity. Hence the hymn writer can say, "Incense breathes a deity nigh." The Hebrew Scriptures contain 129 references to incense used in worship. It was supposed to be pleasant to God's nostrils and was burned in the Temple. The Torah is filled with references to incense. In Malachi, the last book of the Old Testament, this prophet suggests the sign of universalism is that "in every nation incense shall be offered to my name." With the symbolic existence of incense Matthew signals the divine presence met in Jesus.

Finally, Matthew adds myrrh to the gifts brought to Jesus at his birth. Matthew was basing his story on the gospel of Mark. For the first time, Matthew added a birth narrative and then goes on to devote about 40 percent of his gospel to the passion story of Jesus. He began the account of Jesus' final week with the narrative of his triumphant entry into Jerusalem. He then traced the details of his last week culminating in his crucifixion, burial and resurrection. For Matthew it was to be through the death of Jesus that his meaning would be revealed. He felt the need to signal this climax by introducing his death into the story of his birth. That is exactly what the presence of myrrh in the story of the wise men does.

Perhaps we can now understand what Matthew was trying to tell us in the story of the wise men. Essentially he begins his gospel by saying 'let me tell you the story of Jesus.' He was born to be the king of the Jews. That role was to reveal the presence of God in human form through his crucifixion and subsequent resurrection. This was to serve as the transformation of death itself. He does this by turning Isaiah 60 into a narrative of magi or kings coming on camels to the place of Jesus' birth and bringing with them the symbols of Jesus' kingship, Jesus' divine nature and Jesus' death.

I suspect, and this is obviously just a guess, that behind this story lay a sermon, preached in a synagogue by a follower of Jesus, learned in the Hebrew Scriptures. In my mind this sermon was delivered on the Sabbath when the lesson, taken from the latter prophets, came from Isaiah 60. His sermon was an interpretive story. Both he and his audience in the synagogue knew his sermon was never meant to be thought of as literal history.

When Christianity moved out of its Jewish womb and into the Gentile world, however, there was a vast ignorance of the Jewish Scriptures in the Christian Church. They no longer saw the connection between the stories told about Jesus and its Hebrew antecedents. Having no other frame of reference with which to interpret the gospel narratives, these Gentile Christians simply began to literalize the stories. They did this through their art, in sermons, in their hymns and in their liturgy.

Rescuing the Bible from this kind of fundamentalism is now one of the necessary steps Christianity must adopt on its pathway to survival in the 21st century. Being able to see the Jewish antecedents of these stories is the first major step in accomplishing this task.

A few more facts frequently missed the need to be noted by the readers of this gospel, so let me point them out. There is no mention of camels in Matthew's story of the wise men. Camels are only mentioned in Isaiah 60.

Nowhere in Matthew are the wise men said to have been three in number. We read that into Matthew's story from the list of three types of gifts the wise men were supposed to offer. The text of Matthew says that "opening their treasures, they offered him gifts (note the plural) of gold, frankincense and myrrh." It does not say one gold gift, one frankincense gift or one myrrh gift.

Finally, read Matthew's story carefully and you will see the wise men came to a house in Bethlehem over which their guiding star rested. In that house lived Joseph with Mary and her baby. There was no stable. There was no journey from Nazareth to Bethlehem to be enrolled. There was no census ordered by Caesar Augustus when Quirinius was governor of Syria. Those are details from a later source and one that has been blended into Matthew's story.

Our task thus far is to see Matthew's original birth of Jesus story in its actual context. This was the first story of Jesus' birth ever to be written and it did not enter the Christian tradition until the 9th decade CE. About ten years after Matthew's first birth narrative, a second and quite different birth story would be added to the tradition by a gospel writer we call Luke.

Introducing the
Lucan Story

Somewhere from six to ten years after the Gospel of Matthew was written, the gospel we call Luke makes its appearance. Both Matthew and Luke had Mark as a common source. However, Matthew used it more extensively than Luke. Some scholars also believe Matthew and Luke had a second common source, a collection of the sayings of Jesus they call Q. This source, however, has never been discovered in any independent way. Its only existence appears to be in the common usage Matthew and Luke made of it.

There are a few scholars who do not accept the existence of Q as a separate source. They account for the non-Marcan similarities in Matthew and Luke by suggesting these similarities exist because Luke not only had access to Mark, but to Matthew as well. This suggests that what people have called Q is nothing more than Matthew's redaction of Mark.

I will not solve this debate. I just want to identify the issues and state a conviction among most American biblical scholars. There is an overwhelming consensus that there once existed a now lost document called Q. For our purposes, we only need to note there is substantial agreement in content beyond having Mark in common between Matthew and Luke. This also means that where Matthew and Luke diverge sharply, we need to enquire as to why.

At least one of the sources of the primary differences between Matthew and Luke can be found in understanding the audiences for which each gospel was created. Matthew's audience consisted of a much more traditional Jewish community that saw Jesus as the fulfillment of Jewish hopes and dreams. Luke's audience was more a community of dispersed Jews who had adapted significantly to the predominantly Gentile world in which they lived. They saw Jesus in much more universal terms as the one who transcended all human barriers and brought human life into a deeper sense of Oneness.

When we survey the books of the New Testament we discover Matthew and Luke alone provide us with stories about the birth of Jesus. Then we discover these two birth narratives differ significantly from each other, reaching the level of overt contradictions. Matthew introduces the birth narrative with a genealogy of Jesus rooting him deeply in Jewish life and history. Luke introduces his narrative of Jesus' birth with a story set in a Jewish context, but then moves quickly forward to its more universal meaning.

For example, Luke also has a genealogy but he uses it not as a preamble to the birth of Jesus, but as a way to launch Jesus' adult ministry. Unlike Matthew's genealogy beginning with Abraham, the father of the Jews, Luke's genealogy goes back to Adam, the father of the entire human race. Luke's genealogy is a number of generations longer than Matthew's. He also avoids the royal line of kings of Judah, going not from David to Solomon to Rehoboam as Matthew does, but from David to Nathan to Mattatha. The two genealogies also differ as to who was Joseph's father. Matthew says it was Jacob; Luke says it was Heli. Those who try to force the Bible into literal harmony cannot get past these dual genealogies.

Luke also gives us a story of the birth of John the Baptist found nowhere else in the New Testament. The purpose of this particular nativity narrative is to indicate the subservience of John the Baptist to Jesus which Luke does at every point. John's birth was spectacular in that he was born to postmenopausal parents, a repeat of the Abraham and Sarah story. Jesus' birth, however, was even more spectacular in that he was the son of a virgin with the Holy Spirit acting as his father.

When John the Baptist was born, the neighbors all gathered to celebrate his birth. That celebration pales beside what Luke claims transpired when Jesus was born. Angels broke through the darkness of the night sky to celebrate and to announce the birth.

Luke goes so far as to say that while John and Jesus were both in the wombs of their respective mothers, Elizabeth and Mary, the fetus of John actually leapt to salute the fetus of Jesus. Even prior to the birth of either of them, John's secondary role to Jesus' primacy was thus established. In the community for which Luke wrote, this reveals the high probability that there was considerable tension between the movement that grew up around John the Baptist and the movement that grew up around Jesus. Luke was weighing in on that debate in order to claim the priority for Jesus.

As we noted earlier in this narrative, Joseph tends to be the focus of the story in Matthew. The annunciation is made to Joseph in a dream by an unnamed angel. While in Luke, Mary is the focus. In this version the annunciation is made to Mary by a specific angel named Gabriel. This was not in a dream, but in real time.

Luke's story includes a number of songs sung by the principals in the drama, thus turning what might have originally been a nativity play into a kind of operetta. Zechariah, at the birth of his son John, is made to sing the words that have come to be called the *Benedictus*. Mary sings the words we now call *The Magnificat* on her visit to Elizabeth, her kinswoman. She lives, we are told, in the hill country of Judea. The angels sing the words we now call the *Gloria in Excelsis* to the hillside shepherds. Finally, an old priest named Simeon sings the words we know as the *Nunc Dimittis.* This occurs when he sees the baby Jesus for the first time and recognizes him as the fulfillment of the promise for which his entire life had yearned.

While Matthew has Jesus fleeing from the wrath of Herod into the land of Egypt, Luke has him being circumcised on the eighth day after his birth. Following Jewish tradition, he is presented in the Temple 40 days later. He then leisurely makes his way with his family back to his Nazareth home in Galilee. While Luke certainly asserts a virgin status for the mother of Jesus, he never tries to ground that reality in the scriptures of the Jewish people. Once the story of Jesus' birth is told, Luke constantly refers to Joseph as the father of Jesus.

Luke's birth story is by every measure the more popular and best known of the two. Luke's story line, not Matthew's, is followed in our traditional Christmas pageants. These pageants often begin with the appearance of the Angel Gabriel to a virgin in Nazareth causing her to visit Elizabeth in Judea. These pageants then proceed with the journey of Joseph and Mary to Bethlehem to be enrolled. On this journey, Mary is described as being great with child. When they arrive they discover there is no room at the inn. She probably had the baby in the open country and placed him in a conveniently located feeding trough.

No stable is ever mentioned in Luke's text. Human imagination has created the stable and populated it with cows and sheep. No animals are found in Luke's narrative, not even one who says, "Do you see what I see?"

There is no star and there are no wise men in Luke. Luke apparently did not care for magi. In the book of Acts, authored by the same person who wrote the gospel we call Luke, he reveals he has little use for either kings or magi. Matthew's three kings or magi are replaced in Luke by humble shepherds. Matthew's star is replaced by a heavenly host of angels. The symbols Luke employs are not gold for a king, incense for a deity or myrrh to mark Jesus' path toward death. Instead he writes of swaddling clothes and a manger. Luke appears to have taken both of these symbols from the Hebrew Scriptures.

In the apocryphal book known as the Wisdom of Solomon, Israel's most opulent king was made to say, "When I was born, I was carefully swaddled for that is the only way a king can come to his people." The manger, or feeding trough, seems to have been lifted from the first chapter of Isaiah. There the people of Israel are criticized for not knowing they eat from God's feeding trough. They do not recognize that God is the source of everything that sustains them. In this way Luke introduces the story of Jesus by saying that from the moment of his birth this messianic figure will recognize his relationship with and his dependence on the God of Israel. He will be placed in the feeding trough and will relate to God as a symbol of faithfulness, unlike the historic witness of the Jewish nation. Through this Jesus, not only the Jews, but the people of the entire world, will learn of God's infinite love for all God has made.

There is one other echo from the Hebrew Scriptures found in Luke's story of Jesus' birth in the figure of Samuel. In the story of Samuel, his mother, Hannah, is unable to conceive a child. She is found weeping in God' sanctuary by a man named Eli, the high priest. Eli tells Hannah her prayers have been answered and she will bear a son. Consequently, Samuel's birth is also surrounded by supernatural events.

In gratitude Hannah pledges her son Samuel to the service of God. When Samuel is born, Hannah sings a song very similar to *The Magnificat* sung by Mary. Indeed most scholars think *The Magnificat* is based on Hannah's song.

When Samuel is of age, Hannah takes him to the worship center of his nation and dedicates him to the service of God under the tutelage of Eli, the high priest. That story finds an echo in Luke when Mary and Joseph take the 12–year old Jesus to the Temple for Passover, probably in a kind of Bar Mitzvah ceremony. Finally, to return to the genealogy of Luke in which Jesus' relationship to God is publicly announced, we note once again that Luke says the father of Joseph was one named Heli. Heli is the Greek spelling of the Hebrew Eli, the name of the elderly high priest under whom Samuel served. Perhaps in using this name Luke was signaling he was drawing on the story of Samuel to tell his story of Jesus.

The Old Testament Antecedents in Luke's Story of Jesus' Birth

In order to understand the birth narratives found in Matthew and Luke, we need to embrace the fact that there is no way these stories were intended to be regarded as remembered history or as narratives that were literally true. That must be stated clearly. This means there never was a star in the east or wise men who followed it. There never was a heavenly host of angels who sang to hillside shepherds. There never was a miraculous birth.

These stories are memorable, engaging and fanciful, but neither Matthew nor Luke believed themselves to be recording something that actually happened at the time of Jesus' birth. They knew they were creating narratives in which they used symbols to interpret the adult experience the community's leaders had with one named Jesus of Nazareth.

The proof of this is grasped when we discover how much stories from the Hebrew Scriptures, rather than eye witness accounts, were used to provide the context of their birth narratives. Matthew's story of the wise men, for example, was originally the creative work of an imaginative preacher. He combined Isaiah 60 with the story of the visit of the Queen of Sheba to King Solomon (1 Kings 10) with some other illusions from the story of Balaam and Balak (Numbers 22–24). When we turn to Luke's story, we discover time after time he drew on accounts in Genesis with other toe-dips into such sources as the books of Daniel, Exodus and Malachi. It is an exciting adventure to unravel this biblical mystery story.

Luke's narrative begins with the birth of John the Baptist. One knowledgeable of the Hebrew Scriptures will immediately see here a familiar Jewish story. First, the parents of John the Baptist are introduced. Their names are Zechariah, a priest of the order of Abijah, and Elizabeth, a daughter of Aaron. He was both the brother of Moses and the first high priest of the Jewish nation. Both Zechariah and Elizabeth are described as righteous people, who "followed the laws of God in a blameless way."

They were now elderly, childless and thus without an heir. This, in a typically patriarchal way, was blamed on the woman who was called barren. No one knew anything in those days about low sperm counts. Readers familiar with the book of Genesis will recognize this story as a retelling of the Genesis story of Abraham and Sarah prior to the conception of Isaac.

Then the story of John the Baptist unfolds. Zechariah's priesthood responsibility was to perform the sacred functions in the Temple. By lot, the opportunity to burn the incense in the Holy of Holies fell to him. This was considered to be a moment of intense meaning and high honor. A multitude of people waited outside for this ritual to be completed. People are always drawn to moments when mystery fills the air.

Inside, however, Zechariah was delayed by what we are later to learn was a revelatory vision. An angel of the Lord appeared to him standing on the right side of the altar of incense. Zechariah fell away in fear. The angel spoke telling him not to be afraid. His prayers for a child had been heard and Elizabeth would bear a son. This son, the angel says, will accomplish great things working "in the spirit and power of Elijah."

Zechariah is incredulous. "How shall I know that this is so? My wife and I are well advanced in years." In Genesis, Sarah was said to have been 90 years old and past the time of women to produce children. Identifying himself as Gabriel, the angel gives Zechariah a sign. "You will be unable to speak until the child is born." That too elicited Jewish scriptural memories. In the eighth chapter of Daniel, a vision of the Angel Gabriel appeared to Daniel in the Temple. Following this vision he was commanded not to speak. These stories are being replicated by Luke.

This episode took so much time the crowd of worshipers began to wonder what was happening. What went wrong? When Zechariah finally appeared and was unable to speak, their wonder was greatly enhanced. He must have had a vision, it was speculated, but its content was not disclosed to them. Zechariah then completed his priestly duties and returned to his home. There, we are told, Elizabeth conceived and hid herself for five months, while she rejoiced that the Lord has "taken away my reproach among men."

Assuming this story is not history, we ask why Luke decided to name the parents of John the Baptist Zechariah and Elizabeth. Names are always clues in interpretive tales. There are a number of Zechariahs in the Hebrew Scriptures. The most important one is the prophet whose work is recorded in the *Book of the Twelve*, also called the *Minor Prophets.*

Zechariah is the next to last book in the Old Testament followed only by the book of Malachi. Malachi is not the name of the author of this book. Rather it is a Hebrew word that means my messenger. Malachi is thus a nameless voice whose task is to be the messenger, who "prepares the way for the coming of the Lord." The book of Malachi relates this messenger to Elijah. As we noted earlier, the angel tells Zechariah the promised child will come "in the spirit and power of Elijah." If John the Baptist is thus to be identified with Malachi, the nameless messenger who prepares the way for the Lord, then why not signal that fact by giving John's father the name Zechariah, the name of the immediate predecessor of Malachi? Luke sends a message with this name. It was not accidental.

What then about his mother Elizabeth? That is a little more difficult, but not impossible to demonstrate. There is a clue in Luke's text where Elizabeth is said to be a daughter of Aaron. There is only one other Elizabeth in the entire Old Testament where the name is written not Elizabeth but Elisheba. That single Elisheba is the wife of Aaron. This also makes her a sister-in-law to both Moses and his sister Miriam. Miriam plays a major role in the story of the Exodus and a song of triumph is attributed to her after the successful crossing of the Red Sea.

Is Luke going to pattern the family of Jesus after the analogy of the family of Moses? I believe he does and this conviction opens up Luke's interpretive genius. First be aware that in Hebrew, Miriam, when translated, would be Mary. In the entire New Testament only in Luke is there any sense that Jesus and John the Baptist are kin. In the 14th century, John Wycliffe suggested they were cousins. The sole hint of relatedness is found in the story Luke tells of the Annunciation by Gabriel to Mary when she learns she is to be the mother of the Holy Child. Gabriel uses these words, "your kinswoman, Elizabeth, in her old age, has also conceived a son and this is the sixth month with her who was called barren." If Luke's analogy for Elizabeth was Aaron's wife, Elisheba, and if Aaron's sister Miriam was to be Mary, then Elizabeth and Mary were going to be the mothers of these two promised children. One, the first born, was destined to be the forerunner; the other, the second born, the messiah. They would clearly have been first cousins.

Luke then has Mary, pregnant with Jesus, go into the hill country of Judah to visit her kinswoman, Elizabeth, pregnant with John the Baptist. Here one other interpretive experience occurs. There is a fetal salute. The baby in Elizabeth's womb leaps to salute the baby in Mary's womb. This establishes the issue of priority which is settled before the birth of either. What in the world does that mean?

When the gospel of Luke was written there was obviously tension between the Jesus movement and the John the Baptist movement. That tension is recounted in the book of Acts. Jesus originally was a follower of John. John baptized Jesus according to the first three gospels. It was only when John the Baptist was imprisoned that Jesus broke forth as a leader in his own right. Some of Jesus' disciples had come to him after having been disciples of John. The disciples of Jesus felt a need to establish the priority of Jesus. Luke accomplishes this by suggesting there had been a fetal salute establishing Jesus' superiority. From where do you suppose Luke got the idea for that story? Again we turn to the Hebrew Scriptures.

There is only one other story in the entire Bible in which a baby leaps in its mother's womb in a way that meaning is attributed to that movement. It is found in the book of Genesis. In chapter 25, Rebekah, the wife of Isaac was pregnant. When the baby leaped in her womb, she went to an oracle to help her understand what this leaping meant. There she was informed she was having twins. The meaning of the fetal leap was to establish that the first born of the twins, who would be named Esau, would actually serve the second born of the two, who would be named Jacob. Luke takes this Genesis story and transforms it. Jesus and John the Baptist are not twins but they are kin, he suggests. John was the elder by six months, Luke tells us. In this case the elder of the two, John, was to be the servant of the second born, Jesus.

This echoed the destiny of the first born, Esau, who was destined to be the servant of the second born, Jacob. John, who was to prepare the way for Jesus, will later be made to say about Jesus, "He must increase, I must decrease." Luke grounded the John the Baptist story in the Hebrew Scriptures. The vision in the Temple and the inability to speak came from Daniel. The post-menopausal pregnancy comes from Abraham and Sarah. The superiority of Jesus to John, as well as their kinship, comes from the story of Jacob and Esau.

Luke mines the Hebrew Scriptures to portray Jesus' birth. One cannot understand the birth narratives unless one sees their connections with the Hebrew Scriptures.

The Journey to Bethlehem

T he creators of the birth narratives, Matthew and Luke, used two motifs in interpreting the life of Jesus of Nazareth. First, each was historically aware that Jesus hailed from Galilee from the village of Nazareth. Too often the gospels report there was debate about his origins but this is not true. Galilee was the rustic, impoverished, illiterate and non-cultural part of the Jewish nation. Nazareth was an insignificant town in a looked-down-upon region. Yet, they could never escape the fact that Jesus was called Jesus of Nazareth and referred to as a Galilean.

The claim of Jesus' disciples that he was the messiah was ridiculed because of the historical facts of his origin. "Search the scriptures," his critics invited the crowds to do, "and nowhere will you find the suggestion that the messiah will come out of Galilee." It was thought even more impossible for the messiah to grow up in Nazareth. "Nothing good can come out of Nazareth," they declared. History is sometimes quite inconvenient when myth-making is going on. This was the first motif of the birth narratives.

The place of Jesus' origin seems not to have been an issue for Paul. Mark, the first gospel writer, assumes Jesus was born in Nazareth and he grew up there. When his place of origin began to be a problem for those eager to assert the messianic claim, the pressure began to build to locate his place of birth in a more noble setting. That was when the second motif around his birth appeared and had to be served.

There were many messianic images in Jewish history. A major and consistent one was that the messiah had to restore the throne of King David. In time, this meant the messiah had to have a claim to be a descendent and thus an heir to the royal line of King David. That throne was lost to the Jews in 586 BCE. In that year the Babylonian conquerors destroyed Judah in warfare. In the war's aftermath the Babylonians rounded up and murdered all the heirs to the Davidic line. They imprisoned a man named Zedekiah after putting out his eyes. When Zedekiah finally died in prison, the royal throne of the House of David was thus thought to be vacant.

Then the idea of the messiah began to grow both in Jewish thought and in Jewish mythology. The coming of the Messiah was part of the national dream of restoration. The royal line of King David was an important symbol in all the hopes expressed for the coming kingdom. The desire was that the messiah would reflect his Davidic roots by being born in Bethlehem, the city of David. This was read into a text by the prophet Micah that extolled the little town of Bethlehem as the birthplace of Judah's kings.

Slowly, this town, with its royal connections and its location in the land of Judah about six miles from Jerusalem, began to rise in the messianic dreams. The Messiah must be of the house of David and he must be born in Bethlehem.

Matthew was the first to make this claim, but it was easy for him. He assumed both Mary and Joseph lived in a house in Bethlehem. For this baby to be born there seemed quite natural. Matthew's problem was he then had to find a way to deal with actual history. This baby, though born in Bethlehem, would grow up in Nazareth of Galilee.

Luke, who accepts Mark's frame of reference involving Jesus' Galilean roots, had the opposite problem. How could it be arranged for a couple who lived in Galilee to be in Bethlehem when the child was born? Luke hit upon a scheme that probably has some semblance of history to it. He used it to tell his magnificent story so familiar to most of us today.

There went out a decree from Caesar Augustus that all the world was to be enrolled. Was this a census? Was it for the purpose of taxation? We learn from the Old Testament that the Jews periodically wanted to count their citizens. There are historical hints of a census ordered within a decade after the death of King Herod or around 6 to 7 CE. However, the idea that an empire-wide census was ever undertaken stretches credibility to the breaking point. There were no records, no birth certificates, no marriage certificates and no death certificates. There were no records stored anywhere. Travel was hard and slow.

Luke, however, needed to have a hook on which to create his story of the Bethlehem birth of a child whose parents were citizens of Nazareth. So he used the presumed census to account for the fact that Joseph and Mary had to go to Bethlehem.

This enrollment, Luke said, occurred when Quirinius was governor of Syria. That was an interesting addition. Luke has already related that the births of John the Baptist and Jesus had occurred when Herod was the King of Judea. We know from secular records, however, that

Herod died in the year 4 BCE. On the other hand, we know that Quirinius did not become governor of Syria until the winter in which the year 6 CE turned into the year 7 CE. If Jesus was born when Herod was king, he would have been 10 to 11–years old when this enrollment was ordered. The presumed history behind this birth narrative begins to wobble perceptibly.

Next we learn that Joseph, because he was of the house and lineage of David, must, as a prerequisite for this census, return to his ancestral home to be enrolled. This, Luke asserted, was the key that resulted in a Bethlehem birthplace for Jesus.

Does this mean all the direct heirs of King David had to make the journey to Bethlehem? David, who according to the Bible had many wives and many concubines, reigned in Judah from the year 1000 to 960 BCE. If we count a generation at 20 years, a rather generous number in a world where life expectancy was only in the 30's, there would be about 48 generations between David and Jesus. If David had only 50 children, a rather small number for a king with a large harem, his direct descendants in 48 generations would be well over a billion people. Suppose, as Luke asserts, all of David's direct heirs had to return to Bethlehem to be enrolled? It is no wonder there was no room at the inn. Historicity is shattered.

One final note. Luke tells us Joseph had to take Mary with him for this enrollment. Why this was necessary is not stated. In that patriarchal era, women were not enrolled, counted or taxed. They were thought of as property, part of the male's wealth upon which taxes were paid. If this baby is to be born in Bethlehem, however, Mary must be in Bethlehem. So Luke tells us Joseph took her with him even though she was great with child, to use the beautiful language of King James' English. Great with child surely means near to term so we can assume she was in her last month of pregnancy.

How many of us have ever stopped to realize Bethlehem was 94 miles from Nazareth? Do we embrace the idea that the two options for transportation open to them in the first century were walking or riding on a donkey? Do we understand this was a seven to ten-day journey that would have to average nine to 12 miles a day? Are we aware that in this era there were no restaurants or hotels along the way? Now ask yourself, what man in his right mind would take his nine-month pregnant wife on a 94-mile journey? Whether on a donkey or actually walking, the literal reason for taking her does not hold any credibility. It was a Roman Catholic lay theologian, Rosemary Ruether, who after reading this birth narrative in Luke, remarked that "only a man who had never had a baby could have written this story."

Religious art portrays this journey to Bethlehem with Mary riding side saddle on a donkey led by a walking Joseph. That is little more than romantic imagination. In the text there is no donkey. That should not surprise us. In Matthew's story of the wise men, there are no camels. In Luke's story, there is no stable. There are no animals around the Christ Child in the stable because there is no stable. There is only a feeding trough, called a manger. That feeding trough could be out in the fields as easily as it could be inside a structure. Be aware, pageants and human imagination have created images for us that are in fact not biblical.

Luke's story, however, has achieved its agenda. The Nazareth-based family has managed to be located physically in Bethlehem when the child is born. The messianic connection has been established. Mythology has been enhanced.

Luke does two more things mentioned earlier. I repeat them here, because we can see them now in context. He takes a text from the Wisdom of Solomon where the richest of all the Jewish kings says, "When I was born I was carefully swaddled, for there is no other way for a king to come to his people." So Luke says they wrapped the babe in swaddling clothes. This clue was given to the shepherds to help them find him. Second, he was placed into a manger, an image Luke borrowed from Isaiah 1. This one faithful Jew, unlike the history of his people in the time of Isaiah, would know from the moment of his birth who was his father and what largesse he received from the God he represented. There are many levels on which the stories of the birth of Jesus can be read. Literalism is not one of them.

This is rich material, but it is not history. Our analysis reveals it was never understood by the authors of both Matthew and Luke to be history. It is a pity the Gentiles, who became both the majority and the dominant strain in the Christian Church after about 150 CE, did not know the Jewish Scriptures well enough to understand what the original stories meant. Literalism is not only an expression of biblical ignorance, but it is a distortion of the gospel so dangerous as to be destructive of Christianity itself.

Conclusions

Luke concludes his birth story with a series of episodes designed to point to the story of the adult Jesus. First, in Luke's story, the shepherds depart, while Mary ponders. Then the Holy Family goes through the initiation rites of Judaism to root Jesus deeply inside of the faith of his people. He is circumcised, Luke says, on the eighth day and given the name Jesus (Joshua or Yeshuah in Hebrew/Aramaic). He is presented at the Temple on the 40th day. At that time a prophetess named Anna, later to be viewed in mythology as the mother of Mary, and an old priest named Simeon, are introduced in brief cameo appearances. In this baby, Simeon proclaims he has seen the promised salvation that will bring light to the Gentiles and glory to Israel. Next, and in contrast to Matthew, who has the Holy Family flee into Egypt to avoid the wrath of Herod, Luke has them make a rather leisurely journey back to their home in Nazareth. This episode of Luke's birth narrative is then closed with a summary statement informing his readers that "the child grew and became strong, filled with wisdom; and the favor of God was with him." The infancy narrative is thus completed.

Luke then describes an episode that turns out to be the only story in the entire New Testament that purports to inform us about Jesus' childhood. It is the narrative of the 12-year old Jesus being taken up to Jerusalem at the time of the Passover. It is a puberty rite story couched in religious terms; a kind of primitive bar mitzvah filled with familiar mythological content. It was intended to show just how remarkable the child Jesus really was long before his introduction to the wider public as an adult figure. It also has deep roots in the Hebrew Scriptures we need to identify.

Those familiar with these scriptures would also be familiar with the life of the prophet Samuel. He, like Jesus, was said to have had something of a miraculous birth. His mother Hannah was childless; she had been unable to conceive. In that patriarchal world, the woman was blamed for this condition and so she was called barren. She was one of two wives married to a man named Elkanah. His second wife, Peninnah, had children and was honored by her husband because of that. Hannah, however, felt shame at her inability to have a child. She was even ridiculed by Peninnah because, as she said, "the Lord had closed her womb."

Hannah went up regularly to a holy place, the shrine at Shiloh. On one of those occasions, she was at the gate of the shrine weeping and praying for a child. In her prayers she stated her willingness to dedicate her child to God if her prayers were answered. In the emotional power of this prayer, she came to the attention of an old priest named Eli who thought at first that she was drunk.

"How long will you be drunken?" he asks her as the conversation began. Hannah responded, "No, my Lord, I am a woman sorely troubled. I have drunk neither wine nor strong drink, but I have been pouring out my soul before the Lord." Hearing the content of her prayer, Eli promised her prayer would be answered. So he said to her, "Go in peace and may the God of Israel grant your petition." Hannah then returned home and her barrenness was overcome; Samuel was born. It is a touching story.

Luke is clearly familiar with the story of Hannah. When Hannah's child, Samuel, was born, she sang a song of praise that began with the words, "My heart exults in the Lord." Luke uses Hannah's song as the model for the song he puts in the mouth of Mary that we call *The Magnificat.* It begins with the words, "My soul magnifies the Lord."

I believe there is one other oblique reference to the story of Samuel in Luke's birth narrative. In his genealogy of Jesus in chapter 3, Luke lists a person named Heli as the father of Joseph. Thus Heli is the grandfather of Jesus. Heli is simply the Greek spelling of Eli. The old priest in the book of Samuel is related, Luke says, to the life of Jesus. Finally, when Mary and Joseph take the boy Jesus to present him in the Temple when he was 12-years old, Luke appears to base this story on the account of Hannah taking the boy Samuel when he was weaned to the shrine at Shiloh. There he would serve the priest Eli as the fulfill-ment of Hannah's vow to dedicate her son to the service of God. The visit to the Temple completed the cycle of Jewish initiatory liturgies. Luke tells us Jesus was circumcised on the 8th day, presented on the 40th day and dedicated at the age of 12 in the Temple at Jerusalem. The child Jesus was therefore born with the destiny to serve God in all aspects of the Jewish tradition.

This visit to the Temple at age 12 is also filled by Luke with hints of things to come. The boy Jesus claims the Temple for himself in his childhood just as he will do later as an adult. In this episode Jesus acknowledges God as his father. He claims this Temple as his father's house and states he must be about his father's business. In this narra-tive he is also said to have been lost for three days. When he was found, he said he was in his Father's house. This reveals echoes of another three days in which Luke will say he was lost until raised by God into a new dimension of God's presence. His body will then be referred to as the New Temple.

It is interesting to note that Luke then moves imme-diately to the story of Jesus' baptism by John in the River

Jordan and the inauguration of his messianic career. Now Joseph disappears from Luke's text and takes his place in the mythology of the ages out of which he had come in the first place. With this story the birth narratives have completed their purpose. The meaning of Jesus' life has been introduced to his followers. With this story we also reach the end of this chronicle so it is time to summarize.

There is nothing in the birth narratives of Matthew and Luke that was ever intended to be viewed as literal history. Both of these gospel authors knew the birth narratives were designed to explain the source of power experienced in the life of the adult Jesus of Nazareth. Both were trying to say they had met a power and presence in the life of Jesus that human beings could not themselves ever have produced. Both picked symbols out of Hebrew history to flesh out their stories. Both knew they were introducing a new idea into the developing Christian tradition. Both were surely aware their stories of a miraculous birth for Jesus were unknown to Paul. He portrayed Jesus as one who was born of a woman as every human being is, and born under the law as every Jew was. The only special claim Paul made for Jesus was that he "was descended from the House of David, according to the flesh." For Paul, God had declared Jesus to be the son of God, not through a miraculous birth, but through his resurrection from the dead (Romans 1:1–4).

They also knew Mark, whom both Matthew and Luke had incorporated into their gospel accounts, not only had no birth story, but he also stated that God first entered Jesus at his baptism. Mark even portrayed Jesus' mother as thinking the adult Jesus was beside himself or out of his mind (Mark 3) when he came into his adult life. That is not the response of one who has been told in advance her child will be holy, the son of the highest. It is clear both Matthew and Luke were not writing about the literal birth of Jesus. That will be the agenda of the fundamentalists to come much later.

Then we saw how these two evangelists developed their stories out of the Hebrew Scriptures. Matthew borrowed from Isaiah who wrote of kings coming to the "brightness of God's rising." He has them bring gold and frankincense to fashion his narrative of wise men and their guiding star. He adapted a Moses story about a wicked king who tried to destroy God's anointed one at birth for his narrative of Jesus. He has Jesus repeat the life cycle of the Jewish nation by coming out of Egypt. He creates the character of Joseph, Jesus' earthly father, out of the account of Joseph the patriarch in the book of Genesis (37–50). The two Josephs are almost interchangeable.

Luke also borrows images from the Old Testament to describe the birth of John the Baptist. He lifts a story from the book of Daniel to explain how John's father, Zechariah, got the news he was to be a father and why he could not speak. He lifts the account of John's post-menopausal birth out of the Abraham and Sarah story in the book of Genesis. He populates Bethlehem with shepherds because it was the birthplace of David, the Shepherd King. He borrows a text from Isaiah to get his manger and a text from the Wisdom of Solomon to get his swaddling clothes. Both narratives are artfully crafted pieces of haggadic Midrash. No Jewish reader would fail to notice that. The two stories are deeply contradictory if one treats them literally. However, both serve as overtures to the story of the life of Jesus, introducing themes that will be developed more fully in their later gospel accounts.

For most people the birth stories are probably the most familiar part of the New Testament. They are also probably the most misunderstood. They are victimized by the annual Christmas pageants held in most churches. They are distorted by hymns sung, oratorios heard and sermons preached each Christmas season. They are celebrated in lawn crèches built, Christmas cards sent and store windows dressed during the holiday season.

Like all birth stories, however, they are not really about the birth of the hero, but about the adult life of the hero. Once we break them out of their literal prison, they take on a new wonder, a new meaning and a new power. That is what this account has also been designed to do. I hope I have succeeded and the next Christmas season can be entered into with open minds and hearts without the need to defend Jesus from those who think the only way to be true to Jesus is to literalize the words of the New Testament.